TOP 10
MADRID

CHRISTOPHER & MELANIE RICE

EYEWITNESS TRAVEL

Left **Parque del Retiro** Right **Puerta del Alcala**

LONDON, NEW YORK,
MELBOURNE, MUNICH AND DELHI
www.dk.com

Produced by Sargasso Media Ltd, London
Printed and bound in China by Leo
Paper Products Ltd.

First American Edition, 2003
13 14 15 16 10 9 8 7 6 5 4 3 2

Published in the United States by DK Publishing,
345 Hudson Street, New York,
New York 10014

**Copyright 2003, 2013 © Dorling Kindersley
Limited, London
Reprinted with revisions 2007, 2009, 2011, 2013**

A catalog record for this book is available from
the Library of Congress

ISSN 1479-344X
ISBN 978-0-75669-597-2

Within each Top 10 list in this book,
no hierarchy of quality or popularity is
implied. All 10 are, in the editor's opinion,
of roughly equal merit.

MIX
Paper from
responsible sources
FSC™ C018179

Contents

Madrid's Top 10

The information in this DK Eyewitness Top 10 Travel Guide is checked regularly.
Every effort has been made to ensure that this book is as up-to-date as possible at the time of
going to press. Some details, however, such as telephone numbers, opening hours, prices,
gallery hanging arrangements and travel information are liable to change. The publishers
cannot accept responsibility for any consequences arising from the use of this book, nor for
any material on third party websites, and cannot guarantee that any website address in this
book will be a suitable source of travel information. We value the views and suggestions of
our readers very highly. Please write to: Publisher, DK Eyewitness Travel Guides,
Dorling Kindersley, 80 Strand, London, WC2R 0RL, Great Britain or email: travelguides@dk.com

Cover: Front – **4Corners**: SIME/Sandra Raccanello main; **Alamy Images**: Paul Taylor bl. Spine – **Dorling
Kindersley**: Ian Aitken b. Back – **Dorling Kindersley**: Rough Guides/Ian Aitken tr, tc, tl.

Left **Calle Serrano** Right **Terrace café**

Contents

Around Town

Streetsmart

Left **Plaza Mayor** Right **Cibeles fountain**

Key to abbreviations
Adm admission charge **Free** no admission charge **Dis. access** disabled access

3

MADRID'S
TOP 10

MADRID'S TOP 10

TOP 10 Madrid's Highlights

Madrid's three world-class art museums and two royal palaces alone would set the pulses racing, but there is more to this exciting and diverse capital than its tourist sights. The fashion boutiques of the Salamanca district showcase Europe's top designers and are just the tip of a shopping iceberg, perfectly complementing the informality of the fascinating El Rastro market, while Madrid's world-famous tapas bars vie for attention with gourmet restaurants and humble tabernas in a city that never sleeps. To simply watch the world go by, head for the supremely elegant Plaza Mayor.

Palacio Real

The former residence of Spain's Bourbon rulers boasts more rooms than any other palace in Europe. With priceless collections of tapestries, clocks, paintings, furniture, even Stradivarius violins, there is something here for everyone *(see pp8–11).*

Museo del Prado

This world-famous art gallery is Madrid's obvious must-see. The outstanding collections of Spanish and European painting reflect the taste of royal connoisseurs *(see pp12–17).*

Plaza Mayor

This magnificent square, now lined with shops, has been the focal point of the city ever since Madrid became the capital of Spain's world empire in the 16th century *(see pp18–19).*

Monasterio de las Descalzas Reales

When the daughters of Spain's aristocratic families withdrew from the outside world in the 17th century to live a life of devotion, they donated their wealth to this royal convent in the form of fabulous works of art *(see pp20–21).*

Preceding pages **Statue of Felipe III, Plaza Mayor**

El Rastro

The roots of Madrid's famous flea market go back more than 400 years. The location in Lavapiés, one of Madrid's most colourful working-class neighbourhoods, is another plus *(see pp22–3).*

Museo Thyssen-Bornemisza
Madrid was the envy of the world when it outbid the Getty Foundation and other front runners for this priceless collection of European art, which attracts around three quarters of a million visitors every year *(see pp24–7).*

Museo Reina Sofía
No visitor should miss the chance to see Picasso's *Guernica*, the world's most famous 20th-century painting. This fabulous museum also showcases other modern Spanish greats including Salvador Dalí, Joan Miró and Juan Gris *(see pp28–31).*

Chueca

Cortes

Parque del Retiro
Once the preserve of royalty, this beautiful park in the heart of the city is now enjoyed by visitors and *Madrileños* alike *(see pp32–3).*

400 yards 0 metres 400

Museo de América
Spain's fascination with America began with Columbus's voyages in the 15th century, but this museum casts its net wider than the former Spanish colonies to embrace the entire continent *(see pp34–5).*

El Escorial
Set against the stunning backdrop of the Sierra de Guadarrama mountains, Felipe II's awe-inspiring palace and monastery was founded as a mausoleum for Spain's Habsburg rulers *(see pp36–9).*

Palacio Real

Madrid's fabulous Royal Palace, inspired by Bernini's designs for the Louvre in Paris, is one of Europe's outstanding architectural monuments. More than half of the state apartments are open to the public, each sumptuously decorated with silk wall hangings, frescoes and gilded stucco, and crammed with priceless objets d'art. The palace's setting is equally breathtaking. Laid out before the visitor in the main courtyard (Plaza de la Armería) is an uninterrupted vista of park and woodland, stretching from the former royal hunting ground of Casa de Campo to El Escorial (see pp36–9) and the majestic peaks of the Sierra de Guadarrama.

Façade

🔵 The palace can close for official ceremonies without prior warning, so check before you set out. The best time to avoid the queues is early in the morning. On the first Wednesday of the month (Oct–Jun) you can see the grand Changing of the Guard ceremony, which begins at noon. On all other Wednesdays there's a simple ceremony from 11am until 2pm.

• Calle Bailén
• Map J3 • www. patrimonionacional.es
• 91 454 8800
• Open Apr–Sep: 10am–8pm daily; Oct–Mar: 10am–6pm daily; closed 1 May, 9 Sep
• Dis. access
• Adm €10, €5 (concessions), €7 (for a guided tour including visit to picture gallery), free Wed & Thu (Apr–Sep: 5–8pm; Oct–Mar: 3–6pm) for EU citizens

Top 10 Features

1. Façade
2. Main Staircase
3. Hall of Columns
4. Throne Room
5. Gasparini Room
6. Gala Dining Room
7. Royal Chapel
8. Pharmacy
9. Armoury
10. Campo del Moro

Façade
Stand for a few moments on Plaza de Oriente to enjoy the splendour of Sacchetti's façade, gleaming in the sun. Sacchetti achieved a rhythm by alternating Ionic columns with Tuscan pilasters.

Main Staircase
When Napoleon first saw the staircase after installing his brother on the Spanish throne, he said "Joseph, your lodgings will be better than mine", owing to Corrado Giaquinto's fine frescoes.

Hall of Columns
This exquisite room was once the setting for balls and banquets, and is still used for ceremonial occasions. Attractions include Giaquinto's fresco of Charles III shown as the sun god Apollo and superb 17th-century silk tapestries.

Throne Room
This room *(left)* was designed for Charles III by Giovanni Battista Natale as a glorification of the Spanish monarchy. The bronze lions guarding the throne were made in Rome in 1651.

Gasparini Room 5
Named after its Italian creator, this dazzling room *(right)* was Charles III's robing room. The lovely ceiling, encrusted with stuccoed fruit and flowers, is a superb example of 18th-century *chinoiserie*.

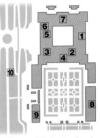

Plan of Palacio Real

Armoury 9
The royal armoury *(below)* has been open to the public for more than 400 years. It boasts more than 2,000 pieces, mostly made for jousts and tournaments rather than the battlefield.

Campo del Moro 10
These beautiful gardens were landscaped in the 19th century and planted with acacias, chestnuts, magnolias, cedars and palms. Stand on the avenue and you'll be rewarded with views of the palace's façade.

Gala Dining Room 6
The banqueting hall *(above)* was created for the wedding of Alfonso XII in 1879. The tapestries and ceiling frescoes are by Anton Mengs and Antonio Velázquez. Look out for the Chinese vases "of a thousand flowers", in the window recesses.

Pharmacy 8
The royal pharmacy was created at the end of the 16th century to supply herbal medicines to the court. Glass retorts, pestles, mortars and jars fill the gilded shelves, while the reconstructed distillery shows how they might have been used.

Building the Palace

The palace stands on the site of the Alcázar, the 9th-century Muslim castle. In 1734 the wooden structure burned down and Philip V commissioned Italian architect Filippo Juvara, then GB Sachetti, to design a replacement. Work began in 1738 and was completed in 1764. The present king, however, prefers to live at the Palacio de Zarzuela outside the city.

Royal Chapel 7
Ventura Rodríguez is usually credited with the decoration of this chapel *(right)*, although he worked hand-in-hand with other collaborators. The dome, supported by massive columns of black marble, is illuminated with some more of Giaquinto's frescoes.

Left **Goya portraits** Right **Porcelain Room**

Top 10 Art Treasures in the Palacio Real

1 Stradivarius Violins

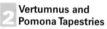
Stradivarius Violin

The priceless "Palace Quartet" (two violins, a viola and violoncello) was made in the 18th century by the world-famous *luthier*, Antonio Stradivari.

2 Vertumnus and Pomona Tapestries

These exquisite tapestries in the Gala Dining Room were made in Brussels by Willem Pannemaker in the mid-16th century.

3 Porcelain

Among the royal porcelain are some fine examples of Sèvres and Meissen dinnerware.

4 Tapestries in the Hall of Columns

These 17th-century tapestries depict scenes from the lives of the Apostles.

5 Goya Portraits

The quartet of portraits by Goya depicting Charles IV and his wife Maria Luisa show the queen as a Spanish *maja* (beauty).

Hall of Columns tapestry

Palacio Real Floorplan

6 Table of the Sphinxes

This 18th-century piece in the Hall of Columns has six bronze sphinxes as table supports.

7 Chronos

This clock was made for Charles IV in 1799; it contains a marble sculpture of Chronos, representing time.

8 Boabdil's Dagger

This beautiful jewelled dagger in the Armoury belonged to the 15th-century Muslim ruler, Mahomet XII (Boabdil).

9 Giaquinto's Apollo

Corrado Giaquinto's fresco on the ceiling of the Hall of Columns shows Charles III as the sun god Apollo.

10 Grandeur and Power of the Spanish Monarchy

Giambattista Tiepolo's frescoes in the Throne Room are a *tour de force*. Marginal figures represent Spain's overseas possessions.

The Habsburgs and the Bourbons

The Austrian house of Habsburg ruled Spain for nearly 200 years (1516–1700), beginning with Carlos I (Emperor Charles V) and his son Felipe II (see p39). By the time the first Bourbon king, Felipe V (grandson of Louis XIV of France), came to the throne, Spain was already in decline. Felipe was immediately challenged by the Habsburg Archduke Charles of Austria, causing the disastrous War of the Spanish Succession (1700–13) which led to Spain losing territories in Belgium, Luxembourg, Italy, Sardinia and Gibraltar. The Bourbon presence also gave Napoleon the excuse to interfere in Spanish affairs, eventually imposing his brother as king. Although the Bourbons were restored (1813), there followed more than a century of political turmoil, during which the dynasty's right to rule was continually challenged until the monarchy was finally abolished in 1931. After the death of the dictator, General Franco, in 1975, his nominated successor, the Bourbon King Juan Carlos I, presided over the restoration of democracy.

Carlos III
One of Spain's most admired and successful rulers was King Carlos III in the late 18th century. His appreciation of the arts and his love of Madrid heralded a second Golden Age for the nation.

The young Juan Carlos (third from left) and the royal family living in exile

Museo del Prado

Housing one of the world's finest art collections, the Prado is one of Madrid's top tourist attractions. At its core is the fabulous Royal Collection of mainly 16th- and 17th-century paintings, transferred from palaces around Madrid. The Prado's strongest suit is Spanish painting, the pick of the artists including Goya with 114 paintings on display and Velázquez with 50. Highlights of the Italian collection (see p14) include masterpieces by Fra Angelico, Raphael, Botticelli, Titian and Tintoretto. The Prado owns over 90 works by Rubens and canvases by other leading Flemish and Dutch artists (see p16). The wing designed by Spanish architect Rafael Moneo in the restored cloister of the Jerónimos church hosts temporary exhibitions and Renaissance sculpture from the permanent collection.

Façade

🛍 There's a museum shop, restaurant and café, which is useful as you can spend all day in the Prado.

🕐 To visit all of Madrid's art highlights buy a ticket for the Art Walk *(El paseo del arte)*, a combined ticket for the Prado, the Thyssen-Bornemisza *(see pp24–7)* and the Reina Sofía *(see pp28–31)*. It's available at all three museums and costs €21.60.

• Paseo del Prado
• Map F5 • 91 330 2800; for advance tickets call 902 10 70 77 • www.museodelprado.es
• Open 10am–8pm Mon–Sat, 10am–7pm Sun & public hols; 6 Jan, 24 & 31 Dec: 9am–2pm
• Adm €12, €6 (concessions), adm + guide €19.50, free 6–8pm Tue–Sat, 5–8pm Sun • Dis. access

Top 10 Spanish Paintings

1. St Dominic Presiding over an Auto-de-Fé
2. The Adoration of the Shepherds
3. Still Life with Pottery Jars
4. Maja Naked
5. Holy Family with Little Bird
6. Las Meninas
7. The Tapestry Weavers
8. The Meadow of St Isidore
9. St Jerome
10. The Third of May 1808: The Shootings on Príncipe Pío Hill

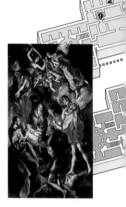

St Dominic Presiding over an Auto-de-Fé

Pedro Berruguete (c.1445–1503) was influenced by the Italians. This painting (c.1495) shows St Dominic sitting in judgment with members of the Inquisition.

The Adoration of the Shepherds

Born in Crete, El Greco (1541–1614) was given his nickname ("The Greek") after settling in Toledo in 1577. This inspirational 1612 masterpiece *(above)* was intended for his own tomb.

Still Life with Pottery Jars

Francisco Zurbarán (1598–1664) was born in Extremadura but trained in Seville. Best known for his religious paintings, this still life (c.1658–64) reveals his

technical mastery in details such as the gleam of light on the pewter dish *(left)*.

For more museums and galleries in Madrid See pp44–5

4 Maja Naked

This famous portrait (c.1797–1800) by Francisco de Goya (1746–1828) is one of the rare nudes in Spanish painting of the time *(right)*. It is one of a pair – the *Maja Clothed* is in the same room for comparison.

9 St Jerome

José de Ribera (1591–1652) painted this expressive portrait of St Jerome (1644). Like many Spanish artists of the period, Ribera was influenced by Caravaggio.

6 Las Meninas

This virtuoso exercise in perspective (1656) is by Diego Velázquez (1599–1660). Flanking the Infanta Margarita *(right)* are her two ladies-in-waiting *(las Meninas)*. The scene also includes the artist, with paintbrush and palette in hand.

7 The Tapestry Weavers

In this superb painting (c.1651) Diego Velázquez's depiction of Madrid upholsterers is also a complex allegory based on the legend of the weaver Arachne.

10 The Third of May 1808: The Shootings on Príncipe Pío Hill

In this dramatic 1814 painting, Goya captures the execution of the leaders of the ill-fated insurrection against the French. The illuminated, Christ-like figure *(see p15)* represents freedom being mowed down by the forces of oppression.

Key

▨	Ground Floor
▨	First Floor
▨	Second Floor

5 Holy Family with Little Bird

Like Zurbarán, Bartolomé Esteban Murillo (1617–82) worked in and around Seville, mainly in the decoration of convents and monasteries. This beautiful work (1650), painted with fluent brushstrokes, is typical of his output.

8 The Meadow of St Isidore

This 1787 Goya landscape *(below)* brilliantly evokes the atmosphere of the San Isidro celebrations *(see p54)* and the clear light of spring.

Museum Guide

The main upper and lower Goya entrances have ticket vending machines outside and ticket desks inside. For disabled access, use the Los Jerónimos entrance and, for educational groups, go to the Murillo entrance. In the Villanueva Building, the second floor has paintings from 1700 to 1800; paintings from 1550 to 1810 are on the first floor; paintings from 1100 to 1910 and sculptures are on the ground floor; and decorative arts are in the basement. The Jerónimos Building has sculptures and temporary exhibitions.

Left **The Story of Nastagio degli Onesti, Botticelli** Right **Annunciation, Fra Angelico**

Italian Paintings in the Prado

1 Annunciation
This superb panel (c.1430) by Fra Angelico (c.1400–55) was presented to the Monasterio de las Descalzas Reales *(see pp20–21)*.

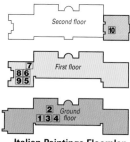

Italian Paintings Floorplan

2 Death of the Virgin
Andrea Mantegna (c.1431–1506) shows the Virgin Mary being carried into heaven in this work (c.1460).

3 The Story of Nastagio degli Onesti
These panels (1483) by Botticelli (c.1444–1510) were commissioned by two rich Florentine families.

4 The Cardinal
This painting (c.1510) by Raphael (1483–1520) is notable for its striking use of colour.

David with the Head of Goliath, Caravaggio

5 The Washing of the Feet
This early work (1547) by Jacopo Tintoretto (c.1518–94) reveals his brilliant handling of perspective.

6 Danäe and the Shower of Gold
Paintings by Titian (1477–1576) were prized by Carlos I. This 1554 work depicts a mythological story by the Latin poet, Ovid.

7 David with the Head of Goliath
Caravaggio (1573–1610) had a major impact on Spanish artists, who admired the dark and light contrasts as seen here (c.1600).

8 The Virgin and Child between two Saints
Founder of the Venetian School, Giovanni Bellini (c.1431–1516) shows an assured use of colour in this devotional painting (c.1490).

9 Venus and Adonis
This beautiful work (c.1580) by Paolo Veronese (1528–88) is a masterpiece of light and colour.

10 The Immaculate Conception
This work (1767–9) by Giovanni Battista Tiepolo (1696–1770) is one of a series intended for a church in Aranjuez.

Top 10 Events in the Life of Francisco de Goya

Francisco de Goya
Spain loves to honour its famous sons and daughters with statuary, as with this figure of Goya outside the Museo del Prado.

Goya's "Black Paintings"

Technically brilliant, irreverent, ironic, satirical, sarcastic and bitter, Goya's "black paintings" are some of the most extraordinary works in the history of art. They originally decorated the rooms of his house, the Quinta del Sordo (Deaf Man's Residence), near the River Manzanares and were produced while he was recovering from a serious illness. In 1873 the then owner of the quinta, Baron D'Erlanger, had the paintings transferred to canvas and donated them to the Prado Museum. What these 14 paintings have in common, apart from the uniformly sombre colour scheme, is a preoccupation with corruption, human misery, sickness and death. The key to the series is the terrifying Saturn devouring his Son, *based on a*

painting by Rubens, but in which the god is transformed from Baroque hero to the incarnation of evil. Even San Isidro Fair, *which features the artist, is almost a travesty of his earlier depiction of the fiesta (see p13) and reveals how far he had travelled as man and artist over the years.*

The Third of May 1808: The Shootings on Príncipe Pío Hill, Francisco de Goya

Left **The Triumph of Death**, Breughel Right **Judith at the Banquet of Holofernes**, Rembrandt

Flemish and Dutch Paintings

1 Descent from the Cross
Felipe II hung this beautiful composition (c.1435) by Rogier van der Weyden (1399–1464) in El Escorial (see pp36–9). It was moved here after the Civil War.

Museo del Prado Floorplan

2 The Garden of Delights
The meaning of this work (1500) by Hieronymus Bosch (c.1450–1516) is hotly debated. The traditional view is that it is a warning against earthly pleasures.

3 The Triumph of Death
This terrifying version of the Dance of Death (c.1562–3) is by Flemish master, Pieter Breughel the Elder (c.1525–69).

4 Portrait of Mary Tudor
Antonis Moor (1519–76) painted this superb portrait in 1554 of the 37-year-old Queen of England, who was to marry Felipe II.

5 Judith at the Banquet of Holofernes
This 1634 painting is the only work in the Prado by Rembrandt (1606–69).

6 The Three Graces
This erotic masterpiece (c.1635) by Peter Paul Rubens (1577–1640) was inspired by classical sculpture and features Love, Desire and Virginity, two of them modelled on wives of the artist.

7 Jordaens Family in a Garden
Jacob Jordaens (1593–1678) was one of the finest portrait artists of the 17th century, as can be witnessed in this 1623 painting.

8 The Artist with Sir Endymion Porter
Anton van Dyck's (1589–1641) 1632–7 portrait is of Endymion Porter, the artist's patron at court.

9 Adoration of the Magi
Rubens first painted this in 1609 but returned to it in 1628 to add three strips that included various figures and his self-portrait.

10 Landscape with Saint Jerome
The attention to the natural detail is a feature of this 1515–19 Joachim Patenier work.

The Artist with Sir Endymion Porter, Van Dyck

Top 10 European Works of Art

1. *Self Portrait*, Albrecht Dürer (German Collection)
2. *Hunting Party in Honour of Charles V in Torgau*, Lucas Cranach the Elder (German Collection)
3. *St Paula Romana embarking at Ostia*, Claude Lorraine (French Collection)
4. *The Parnassus*, Nicolas Poussin (French Collection)
5. San Idelfonso statues (Classical Sculptures)
6. Madrid Venus (Classical Sculptures)
7. Venus of the Shell (Classical Sculptures)
8. Statue of Demeter (Classical Sculptures)
9. Onyx salt cellar with Mermaid (Dauphin's Treasure)
10. The Hunt Vessel (Dauphin's Treasure)

Further European Highlights in the Prado

The highlight of the small but valuable German Collection (room 55B ground floor) is Albrecht Dürer's Self Portrait of 1498, one of a quartet of paintings by this Renaissance master, and his depictions of Adam and Eve. Most of the French Collection dates from the 17th and 18th centuries (first floor, rooms 2–4). Outstanding are the landscapes of Claude Lorraine and the work of Nicolas Poussin. Felipe II began collecting Classical sculptures (ground floor, rooms 71–4) in the 16th century, mostly Roman copies of Greek originals. Look out for the three Venuses – Madrid Venus, Venus of the Shell, Venus of the Dolphin – and the priceless San Idelfonso group, dating from the reign of the Emperor Augustus (1st century AD). The Dauphin's Treasure (basement) was inherited by Felipe V, heir presumptive to Louis XIV of France. The fabulous collection of goblets, glasses and serving dishes was made from precious stones (jasper, lapis lazuli, agate and rock crystal) and encrusted with jewels.

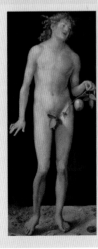

European Portraiture
Albrecht Dürer's lovestruck image of Adam *(left)* is classical in its style, whereas British artist Sir Thomas Lawrence's portrait *(above)* of Miss Marthe Carr illustrates a more realistic leaning.

Plaza Mayor

Madrid's most famous square was built on a grand scale. Capable of holding up to 50,000 people, it was intended to impress and still does. Nowadays it's a tourist attraction first and foremost: a place for relaxing over a drink and watching the world go by. Originally known as Plaza de Arrabal ("Outskirts Square") because it lay outside the city walls, Plaza Mayor was completed in 1619. Following a fire in 1791, Juan de Villanueva (architect of the Prado) redesigned the square, adding the granite archways that now enclose it. During its history, Plaza Mayor has been a market, an open-air theatre, a bullring, a place of execution and a backdrop for tournaments. Its buildings are now mainly used by the city government.

Arcade shops

🍴 Stock up for a picnic on one of the square's benches in the nearby Mercado de San Miguel *(see p49)*.

🕐 The painted enamel street signs for which Madrid is famous provide a clue to the original inhabitants, such as Calle de los Botoneros (Button-makers' Street).

One of the city's main tourist offices is located at Plaza Mayor 27: (91 588 1636), open 9:30am–8:30pm daily.

- Map M5
- Dis. access
- Free
- Metro Sol, Opera

Top 10 Features

1. Statue of Felipe III
2. Casa de la Panadería
3. Casa de la Panadería Murals
4. Casa de la Carnicería
5. Arco de Cuchilleros
6. Cava San Miguel
7. Arcade Shops
8. Terrace Bars and Restaurants
9. Lampposts
10. Stamp and Coin Market

Statue of Felipe III

This magnificent statue *(below)* by two Italian artists, Pietro Tacca and Giambologna, was moved here in the 19th century. Presented to Felipe III in 1616 by the Florentine ruler Cosimo de' Medici, it was originally in the Casa de Campo.

Casa de la Panadería

This house *(above)* was the headquarters of the bakers' guild, which had enormous power controlling the price of grain. The portal survives from the original building which burned down in 1672.

Casa de la Panadería Murals

In the 1980s it was decided that the façade murals were past saving and a competition was held for a new design. The winner, Carlos Franco, painted allegories of the zodiac signs in 1992.

Casa de la Carnicería

This building *(below)* was erected in 1617 and was originally the meat market. It is now used by the Central District Government (Junta Municipal del Distrito de Centro).

Arco de Cuchilleros

"Cutlers" Arch *(centre)* is a reminder of the sword-makers and knife-grinders who once plied their trades here. Today the street is famous for *mesones* (taverns) such as Las Cuevas de Luis Candelas, named after a 19th-century bandit said to have hidden in its cellars.

Cava San Miguel

When the houses were built on this street adjacent to Plaza Mayor, huge quantities of earth were removed from the foundations of the square. To prevent its collapse, frontages on the Cava were designed as sloping buttresses.

Arcade Shops

Buying and selling has always been the life blood of Plaza Mayor. At El Arco de los Cuchilleros (No. 9) all the items on sale have been made by local artisans, continuing a centuries-old tradition.

Terrace Bars and Restaurants

Bars and restaurants put out tables in the summer months *(above)*, and relaxing over a drink is the best way to appreciate the square. Look out for the speciality *bocadillo de calamares* (bread roll filled with squid).

Lampposts

The modern lampposts around the statue of Felipe III are engraved with scenes depicting life on the square in days gone by *(above)*. They include a masquerade ball, an interrogation by members of the Inquisition and a bullfight.

Stamp and Coin Market

Something of a tradition, this market takes place every Sunday morning from around 10am to 2pm and attracts amateur and expert collectors from all over Spain. Otherwise enthusiasts should head for the specialist shops on Calle Felipe III, Calle Mayor and outside the Arco de Toledo.

Auto-de-Fé

The cellars of Moore's Irish bar (Calle Felipe III) were once used by the Inquisition to torture the accused until they confessed to heresy, witchcraft and a multitude of other crimes. Once condemned, they had to undergo a ceremony known as the *auto-de-fé* before being handed over to the secular authorities for punishment. This macabre spectacle, which included a ritual procession and public humiliations, lasted from dawn to dusk. The Plaza Mayor witnessed four *autos-de-fé* between 1624 and 1680.

Monasterio de las Descalzas Reales

This award-winning museum is also a working convent – a haven of peace and quiet after the noise and bustle of Puerta del Sol and the Gran Vía nearby. The building started out as a palace, owned by the royal treasurer, Alonso Gutiérrez, but in 1555 he sold it to the sister of Felipe II, Juana of Austria, who founded the convent four years later. The nuns were Franciscans, but became known, because of their aristocratic backgrounds, as the "Barefoot Royals". The convent is crammed with works of art – paintings, frescoes, sculptures, tapestries, tiles, woodcarvings, embroidered vestments, liturgical gold and silverware – donated by the nuns' wealthy relatives. The church (rarely open to the public) contains the tomb of Juana of Austria.

Façade

🕙 The guided tour lasts for 1 hour, and it is advisable to book well in advance as places on the tour are limited. While all the commentary is given in Spanish only, questions in English are welcomed.

• Plaza de las Descalzas Reales 3 • Map M3
• 91 45 48800 • www.patrimonionacional.es
• Open 10am–2pm, 4–6:30pm Tue–Sat, 10am–3pm Sun & public hols; closed 2 May, 9 Sep • Adm €7, €4 (concessions)

Top 10 Features

1. Grand Staircase
2. Royal Balcony
3. Chapel of the Virgin of Guadalupe
4. Tapestry Room
5. Upper Cloister
6. Antechoir
7. Candilón (Funeral Room)
8. Choir
9. Chapter House
10. Hall of Kings

Grand Staircase

Nothing prepares visitors for this extra-ordinary sight. The Grand Staircase *(right)* belongs to the original palace, but the dazzling frescoes and *trompe-l'oeil*, covering walls, arches and balustrades, were added in the 17th century.

Royal Balcony

As you climb the staircase, look right and you'll see another *trompe-l'oeil* feature. On the "balcony" are Felipe IV and his family – Mariana of Austria, the Infanta Margarita Teresa and the Prince of Asturias, Felipe Próspero. The prince dates the painting by Antonio Pereda, as he died, aged four, in 1661.

Chapel of the Virgin of Guadalupe

The 68 panels *(below)* by Sebastián Herrera Barnuevo feature matriarchs of the Old Testament. The Virgin of Guadalupe painting is a 16th-century replacement.

4 Tapestry Room

The magnificent collection of tapestries, on display in the former nuns' dormitories, were made in Brussels in the 17th century. The 10 panels on view represent the Triumph of the Eucharist.

Plan of the Monasterio de las Descalzas Reales

1 Ground floor
First floor
2
5 3
9 Basement
7 10
6 8
Second floor
4

6 Antechoir

Visitors enter through an intricately carved Plateresque doorway. Among the paintings lining the walls of the three chapels is a beautiful *Virgin and Child* from the late 15th century – one of the oldest works of art in the convent.

7 Candilón (Funeral Room)

By tradition, when a nun died her body was placed on the tiled bier, while prayers were said under the light of a large lamp *(candil)*. The royal portraits *(right)* include two of Felipe II's children and Juana of Austria, both by the 17th-century artist Alonso Sánchez Coello.

8 Choir

The choir *(below)* contains the tombs of Empress María of Austria (sister of Juana) and the Infanta Margarita. One portrait over the entrance is known as the "abandoned girlfriend" – the sitter, María of Portugal, was betrothed to Felipe II but he married Mary Tudor of England instead.

9 Chapter House

The highlight here is a series of 16th-century frescoes depicting the life of St Francis of Assisi. Look out for two devotional works by Pedro de Mena: *Ecce Homo* and *La Dolorosa*.

10 Hall of Kings

This portrait gallery was once used by members of the royal family as a retreat.

Renaissance Music

Today the convent is famous for its artistic treasures, but in the 16th century it was equally renowned for its music. This was largely due to the reputation of Tomás Luis de Victoria, chaplain to the Empress María from 1586 to his death in 1611. Born in Avila, Victoria studied music in Rome, but his output is infused with a mysticism more typical of the Spanish Counter-Reformation. Victoria's religious music was among the first to be heard in the New World.

5 Upper Cloister

The tiny chapels surrounding the cloister *(above)* were rooms of the original palace. Outstanding among the 16th- and 17th-century works of art is a wooden polychrome *Recumbent Christ* by Gaspar Becerra.

🔟 El Rastro

This colourful street market in one of the city's oldest working-class neigh-bourhoods has been going for well over 100 years. The word rastro *means "trail" and refers to the animal innards that were dragged through the streets in the days when this was the site of the main abattoir. The artist Francisco de Goya immortalized the street types here in paintings such as* Blind Man with Guitar, *while earlier it had been the backdrop for comic satires by playwrights of the Golden Age. Among the most exotic inhabitants were the amazonas, a team of horsewomen who performed at royal receptions in the 16th century and are remem-bered in Calle Amazonas. The Rastro is best known for its flea market, the most famous in Spain, but there are also dozens of stalls selling new clothes, furniture and antiques.*

Market stalls

🔵 While Sunday is the main trading day, some stallholders set out their wares on Saturdays too.

The Rastro is a happy hunting ground for thieves and pickpockets so keep a close eye on your valuables at all times.

- Map C5
- Open 8:30am–3pm Sun
- Dis. access
- Free
- Metro La Latina

Top 10 Features

1. Calle Ribera de Curtidores
2. Statue of Eloy Gonzalo
3. Plaza General Vara de Rey
4. Calle Carlos Amiches
5. Calle Mira el Sol
6. Plaza Campillo Mundo Nuevo
7. Calle del Gasómetro
8. Off Ribera de Curtidores
9. Eating in El Rastro
10. Puerta de Toledo

1 Calle Ribera de Curtidores

The Rastro's main street is named after the *curti-dores* (tanners) who once plied their trade here. You can still pick up a leather jacket on one of the dozens of stalls *(below)*, as well as T-shirts, belts, handbags and hats.

2 Statue of Eloy Gonzalo

At the siege of Cascorro in Cuba (1898) Eloy Gonzalo volunteered to start a blaze in the enemy camp and was fatally wounded. Look closely at the statue and you'll see the petrol can.

3 Plaza del General Vara de Rey

Second-hand clothes, candelabras, books and old furniture are on offer on this bustling square *(above)*.

For more markets in Madrid **See p49**

Calle Carlos Arniches

Dropping away from the square, this street *(below)* marks the beginning of the flea market proper. Among the bric-à-brac are watches, cameras, rugs, hats, oil lamps and record players. The lock vendor and his dog are a regular fixture.

Calle del Gasómetro

Car owners may find what they're looking for here: there's usually a good selection of anti-theft locks, windscreen wipers, brake lights and tools. There's also a brisk trade in used computer parts and bicycle accessories.

Eating in El Rastro

There are many bars and cafés in the area. Malacatín *(above)* at Calle Ruda 5 rustles up the delicious local stew *cocido madrileño (see p62)*.

Puerta de Toledo

This triumphal arch *(below)* was unveiled in 1827 and dedicated to Fernando VII. Ironically it had first been proposed during the French occupation to extol the values of liberty and democracy.

Calle Mira el Sol

The place to head to if you're after something electrical, including spare parts, mobile phones and car radios of doubtful provenance. The corner with Ribera de Curtidores is the favourite pitch of the *organillera* (lady organ-grinder), one of the market's more colourful characters.

Plaza Campillo Mundo Nuevo

Adult collectors and children are the main customers, browsing the stacks of old comics and magazines in the vicinity of this square *(right)*. You'll also find CDs, vinyl records, toys and oddities such as binoculars and magnifying glasses.

Off Ribera de Curtidores

Art equipment and picture frames are the speciality of Calle San Cayetano. Stalls near the Army & Navy store on Calle Carnero sell sports gear. Pet owners head for Calle Fray Ceferino González for the miscellany of dog collars, fishing nets and bird cages.

Río Manzanares

The streets of the Rastro lead down to one of Madrid's most neglected features. The Manzanares River is famous only for being short on water and has been the butt of jokes since time immemorial. Until late in the 19th century, its banks were the haunt of washerwomen *(lavanderas)*, colourful figures who appear in the paintings of Francisco de Goya. The Baroque bridge dates from 1719–32. In the middle are sculptures of Madrid's patron saint, San Isidro. Carnations are hung here on his feast day.

Museo Thyssen-Bornemisza

One of the most important art collections in the world, the Thyssen-Bornemisza focuses on European painting from the 13th to the 20th centuries and is the perfect complement to the Prado (see pp12–17) and Reina Sofía (see pp28–31). Wealthy industrialist Baron Heinrich Thyssen-Bornemisza began acquiring Old Masters in the 1920s for his villa in Switzerland. After the baron's death in 1947 his son, Hans Heinrich, added modern masterpieces, including French Impressionists, German Expressionists and the pick of the Russian Avant-Garde (see pp26–7), to the collection. In 1993 the state bought the 1,000-strong collection for the knock-down price of $350 million (the true value being estimated at nearer $1 billion). In 2005 an extension opened, displaying Baroness Carmen Thyssen-Bornemisza's collection, which includes important Impressionist works.

Façade

🍴 The café-restaurant has magnificent views of the garden.

🕐 The Thyssen opens for evening showings in summer, when you can dine at the garden restaurant.

- Paseo del Prado 8
- Map F4 • 902 760 511
- www.museothyssen. org • Open 10am–7pm Tue–Sun (Jul–Aug: to 11pm Tue–Sat); closed 1 Jan, 1 May, 25 Dec
- Adm €9 (or €13 for both the permanent & temporary collections)
- Dis. access

Top 10 Paintings

1. Christ and Woman of Samaria at the Well
2. Self-Portrait
3. Young Knight in a Landscape
4. View of Alkmaar from the Sea
5. The Virgin of the Dry Tree
6. Expulsion, Moon and Firelight
7. Still Life with Cat and Rayfish
8. Portrait of a Young Man
9. The Annunciation
10. Portrait of Giovanna Tornabuoni

Christ and Woman of Samaria at the Well

Outstanding among the collection of Italian Primitives is this work (1310–11) by Sienese master Duccio di Buoninsegna (c.1278–1319). The painting's life-like quality *(above)* reveals Duccio's interest in accuracy and looks forward to the Renaissance.

Self-Portrait

This self-portrait (c.1643) by Rembrandt (1606–69) is one of more than 60 such works by the great Dutch artist. It reveals Rembrandt's view of himself as isolated genius.

Young Knight in a Landscape

Vittore Carpaccio (c.1460– 1525) is an important representative of the Venetian school. This intriguing work (1510) shows a courtly knight amid symbolic animals and plants.

4 View of Alkmaar from the Sea

Dutch artist Salomon van Ruysdael's (1600–70) evocative seascape (c.1650) is one of the finest examples of the genre, for its effortless mastery of colour and perspective.

5 The Virgin of the Dry Tree

This devotional painting (c.1450) by Dutch artist Petrus Christus (c.1410–72), was inspired by an Old Testament metaphor in which God brings the dry tree (the chosen people) to life. The "A"s hanging from the tree stand for Ave Maria and were meditational.

Key

▨	Ground Floor
▨	First Floor
▨	Second Floor

6 Expulsion, Moon and Firelight

This haunting work (c.1828) is by the influential American artist, Thomas Cole, founder of the Hudson River School. Cole idealized the untramelled American landscape as a new Garden of Eden.

7 Still Life with Cat and Rayfish

This witty still life (c.1728) in the Dutch style is by French artist, Jean-Baptiste-Siméon Chardin (1699–1779). Its companion piece, *Still Life with Cat and Fish*, is in Room 27.

8 Portrait of a Young Man

The subject of this painting (c.1515) by Raphael (1484–1520), one of the great artists of the High Renaissance, is thought to be Alessandro de Medici (left), nephew of Pope Clement VII. This haughty youth later became a tyrant and was murdered by his cousin in 1537.

9 The Annunciation

Distorted figures, swirling lines and bold colours (left) are typical of the Mannerist style which El Greco (1541–1614) mastered in Venice, where he was influenced by Titian and Tintoretto, both masters of the High Renaissance. This intensely spiritual painting (c.1567–1577) reveals the Cretan artist's development following his move to Toledo, Spain, in 1577.

10 Portrait of Giovanna Tornabuoni

This sublime portrait (1488) by Florentine painter Domenico Ghirlandaio (1449–94), was the last Baron Thyssen's favourite. It was commissioned to celebrate the marriage of Giovanna degli Albizzi to Lorenzo Tornabuoni – a union of two powerful families. Tragically, Giovanna died in child-birth shortly afterwards.

Museum Guide

The main entrance is through the courtyard where there is a shop and cloakrooms. The collection is organized chronologically, starting with the galleries on the top floor. Visitors following the official route will trace the history of western art, starting with the Italian Primitives and ending with 20th-century abstract and Pop Art. The Carmen Thyssen Collection occupies the first and second floors of the extension. Temporary exhibitions are held on the ground floor and there is a viewing terrace on the fifth floor.

Left **Woman with a Parasol in a Garden**, Renoir Right **Les Vessenots**, Van Gogh

Top 10 Modern Paintings in the Thyssen

1 Woman with a Parasol in a Garden

This Impressionist painting of a garden bathed in sunlight (c.1873) is by one of the founders of the influential movement, Pierre-Auguste Renoir (1841–1920). Renoir was apprenticed for four years as a porcelain painter, and later attributed his technical brilliance in handling surface and texture to his early training.

2 Swaying Dancer

This exquisite study of a dancer in performance (1877–9) by French artist Edgar Degas (1834–1917) is one of a series of his works devoted to the ballet. Unlike some Impressionist painters, Degas placed great emphasis on the importance of drawing, as the superb draughts-manship of this pastel clearly shows.

3 Les Vessenots

Vincent Van Gogh (1853–90) painted this dazzling landscape (1890) during the last year of his troubled life. He worked feverishly while staying at Les Vessenots, near Auvers in France, producing more than 80 canvases in less than three months.

4 Fränzi in Front of a Carved Chair

Ernst Ludwig Kirchner (1880–1938) was an important figure in German Expressionism and a member of the group known as *Die Brücke* (The Bridge), which began the movement in Dresden. These artists were more interested in expressing feelings through their work, and encouraging emotional responses from their audience, rather than portraying outward reality. Fränzi, seen in this lovely 1910 work, was one of their favourite models.

Swaying Dancer, Degas

5 The Dream

A founder member, with Wassily Kandinsky, of the influential *Blaue Reiter* (Blue Rider) group, German artist Franz Marc (1880–1916) took Expressionism in a new, spiritual direction. Colours, as in this 1912 work, are used symbolically, as are the animals in his paintings, which represent truth, beauty and other ideals.

Share your travel recommendations on traveldk.com

6 Still Life with Instruments

Liubov Popova (1889–1924) was one of the most innovative artists working in Russia on the eve of the Revolution. This Cubist painting (1915), completed after a period of study in Paris, paves the way for her *Painterly Architectonic*, an even bolder abstract work exhibited in Room 41.

7 Hotel Room

In this moving 1931 painting by American artist Edward Hopper (1882–1967) the bare furnishings, discarded suitcase and disconsolate posture of the woman holding the railway timetable masterfully suggest loneliness and dislocation – a subject the artist returned to time and again. Hopper is the most important representative of the American social realist school, created in the wake of the Wall Street Crash of 1929 and the Great Depression which followed.

8 New York City, New York

Piet Mondrian (1872–1944) was one of the most influential abstract artists of the 20th century. Born in The Netherlands, he moved to New York after the outbreak of World War II. The simple geometrical forms and bold colours of this abstract painting (1940–42) celebrate the energy and dynamism of his adopted home.

9 Brown and Silver I

Famous for his "action paintings" – randomly throwing or pouring paint onto the canvas in an effort to create spontaneity – Jackson

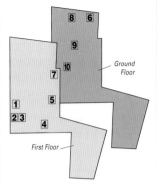

Modern Paintings Floorplan

Pollock (1912–56) made a huge impact on postwar art in America. This painting (c.1951) is typical of the artist's revolutionary approach.

10 Portrait of Baron H.H. Thyssen-Bornemisza

This revealing study of the museum's benefactor (1981–2) is the work of Britain's most distinguished portrait artist, Lucian Freud (b.1922). In the background is *Pierrot Content* by Jean-Antoine Watteau (1684–1721), which visitors will find in Room 28.

Hotel Room, Hopper

📖10 Museo Reina Sofía

The Reina Sofía's collection of 20th- and 21st-century Spanish art is exciting and challenging by turns. The museum, set in a converted hospital, was inaugurated by King Juan Carlos and Queen Sofía in 1992 and, besides the permanent collection, stages outstanding temporary exhibitions from around the world. While most visitors home in on the rooms exhibiting the great masters of the interwar period – Juan Gris, Joan Miró, Salvador Dalí and Pablo Picasso, whose Guernica is the centrepiece of the gallery (see p31) – lesser-known Spanish painters and sculptors are worth seeking out. Works by the European and American avant-garde provide an international context. Exhibits in the permanent collections are susceptible to change.

🍴 The café-restaurant on the ground floor of the Nouvel Building has a daily set-price menu and is accessed from Calle Argumosa 43.

🛍 The museum shop sells Spanish designer jewellery and ceramics as well as books, slides and posters.

• Calle Santa Isabel 52
• Map F6 • 91 774 1000
• www.museoreina sofia.es
• Open 10am–9pm Mon, & Wed–Sat, 10am–2:30pm Sun; closed Tue, 1 Jan, 6 Jan, 1 May, 15 May, 9 Nov, 24–25 Dec, 31 Dec • Adm €6 (free Mon–Fri 7–9pm, Sat after 2:30pm & Sun); Paseo del Arte €21.60
• Dis. access

Top 10 Paintings

1. Woman in Blue
2. Food on the Grass II
3. Portrait of Sonia de Klamery
4. The Gathering at Café de Pombo
5. Bulls (Bullfighting)
6. Portrait II
7. The Great Masturbator
8. Accident
9. Superimposition of Grey Matter
10. Guitar in Front of the Sea

1 Woman in Blue
This marvellous Blue-period portrait (1901) by Pablo Picasso (1881–1973) was painted shortly after his first visit to Paris – he painted the insolent-looking courtesan from memory. When the painting failed to win a national exhibition, a disgruntled Picasso discarded it. It was discovered several years later.

2 Food on the Grass II
Miquel Barceló has created some of Spain's most sought-after contemporary art. While living in Mali in Africa, his paintings were greatly influenced by the desert landscapes and featured elements of this stark environment. The effect of the Sahel's blinding light is clearly seen in his series of white paintings, of which *Food on the Grass II* forms part.

3 Portrait of Sonia de Klamery
Hermengildo Anglada-Camarasa (1871–1959) had a sensual style as this evocative painting (c.1913) shows.

The museum regularly loans works of art to galleries around the world, so not all works may be on display at the time of your visit.

4 The Gathering at Café de Pombo

José Gutiérrez Solana (1886–1945) loved to record the social life of the capital, as in this 1920 portrait. The painting's owner, Ramón Gómez de la Serna, is shown in the centre.

5 Bulls (Bullfighting)

Benjamin Palencia (1894–1980) evokes the arid landscape of La Mancha, while the animals appear symbolic.

6 Portrait II

Joan Miró (1893–1983) encompassed Cubism and Surrealism but he never lost his extraordinary originality. In this 1938 work *(right)* the Catalan painter is more interested in juxtaposing colours rather than revealing the physical attributes of the sitter.

7 The Great Masturbator

Catalan artist Salvador Dalí (1904–89) was a leading exponent of Surrealism, with its exploration of the subconscious. The figure of the Masturbator (1929) is derived from a weird rock formation at Cadaqués.

8 Accident

Also known as *Self-portrait*, Alfonso Ponce de León's (1906–36) disturbing work *(below)*, painted in his last year, prefigured his tragic death in a car crash. The painting, which shows a man violently thrown from a vehicle, is a mixture of realistic elements, lack of depth, flat colour and artificial lighting, which reflect the artist's use of both Surrealism and Magic Realism.

9 Superimposition of Grey Matter

Antoní Tàpies's (b.1923) "matter paintings" explore texture and are composed by adding layers of mixed media, such as sand, powdered marble and paint, onto a pre-varnished canvas.

10 Guitar in Front of the Sea

Juan Gris (1887–1927) became one of Cubism's leading exponents. This 1925 work *(above)* is an excellent example.

Gallery Guide

The entrance to the main Sabatini Building is in Calle Santa Isabel. Permanent collections can be found on the first, second and fourth floors and temporary exhibitions on the first and third floors. Further permanent collections are in the Nouvel Building *(see photo bottom of p28)*. To the west and south of the courtyard are two buildings housing an art library, a restaurant, a book shop and an auditorium.

Left **Toki-Egin** Right **A sculpture gallery**

Sculptures in the Reina Sofía

1 Daphne
From the mid-1920s, Julio González (1876–1942) developed a sculpting language by working with metals using industrial construction methods. *Daphne* (1937) is a defining piece that showcases the possibilities that this new artistic language had to offer.

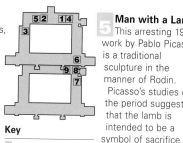

Key

Second Floor

Fourth Floor

2 Great Prophet
Catalan artist Pablo Gargallo (1881–1934) was one of the most important Spanish sculptors during the 1920s and 1930s. He spent nearly 30 years planning this 1933 masterpiece which was sadly only cast after his death.

3 Portrait of Joella
This beautiful sculpture-painting (1933–4) was the fruit of a collaboration between Catalan Salvador Dalí and the leading American Surrealist, Man Ray (1890–1978). Man Ray fashioned the head, leaving Salvador Dalí to add the striking painted dream landscape.

4 Seated Woman I
Born in Barcelona, Julio González (1876–1942) became an apprentice welder in Paris and his training at the forge had a major impact on his work. This abstract piece from 1935 is very typical of his output.

5 Man with a Lamb
This arresting 1943 work by Pablo Picasso is a traditional sculpture in the manner of Rodin. Picasso's studies of the period suggest that the lamb is intended to be a symbol of sacrifice.

6 Sailor with Guitar
Born in Lithuania, Jacques Lipchitz (1891–1973) fell under the spell of Cubism during his first stay in Paris in 1909. This piece (1917) is representative of his Cubist sculptures.

7 Empty Suspension
Jorge de Oteiza (1908–2003) is a highly original Basque sculptor, more interested in form than in expressing feelings or symbols. This forged steel sculpture (1957) was developed around the time the artist was taking an interest in American megalithic statuary.

8 Neo-Concrete Column No 3
Franz Joseph Weissmann (1911–2005) was one of Brazil's leading Modernist sculptors and a member of the Concrete Group. This sculpture (1957) is typical of his geometric abstractions inspired by the Dutch de Stijl movement and consists of intersecting planes of metal.

Woman in Garden

In the late 1920s, Picasso began to frequent the studio of Catalan painter and sculptor Julio González in Paris. During this time, Picasso was inspired to develop his own metal sculpting techniques. He created a number of interesting sculptures, including this remarkable bronze *Woman in Garden* (1930–32), notable for its Surrealist elements.

Toki-Egin (Homage to St John of the Cross)

Eduardo Chillida (1924–2002) is one the most highly regarded sculptors in Spain. This enormous iron construction (1989–90) weighs 9,000 kg (17,500 lbs) – special cranes were needed to install it in the garden. Chillida was a founding member of Grupo '57, an artistic group under the Franco regime.

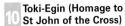

Top 10 Features in Picasso's Guernica

1. Bull
2. Wounded Horse
3. Bereaved Mother
4. Dead Child
5. Dead Soldier
6. Candle
7. Light Bulb
8. Broken Dagger
9. Window
10. Eyes

Guernica's Symbolism

The dismembered bodies, staring eyes, rearing horses gripped in pain, and desperate outstretched arms, combined with the bleakness of a monochrome colour scheme, embody the artist's view of war.

Pablo Picasso's Guernica

On display in Room 206 of the museum is its most precious and famous work. Commissioned as propaganda, Guernica instantly transcended its original purpose. In April 1937, at the height of the Civil War, German bombers devastated the Basque town of Guernica (Gernika) in support of General Franco's Nationalist forces. The attack, almost unprecedented, on a defenceless civilian population caused international outrage. Picasso completed his huge canvas in just two months and it was first exhibited at the Paris World's Fair. Ever since, the meaning and content of Guernica have been minutely analysed, to the irritation of the artist. Picasso chose not to depict the bombardment – there are no aeroplanes, for example – but to indict war, with all its senselessness and barbarity, conceived in terms of the artist's highly individual language of symbols. The preliminary sketches (on display in the adjacent rooms) are a help in understanding the painting. Picasso tried eight different versions before arriving at his ultimate vision.

Guernica

🔟 Parque del Retiro

The Retiro is the city's green lung and the madrileños' favourite weekend retreat. The aristocracy was first admitted to the former royal grounds in 1767 but it was another century before the gates were opened to the general public. Visitors can enjoy not only the decorative features, which include statues and sculptural arrangements, follies, a formal French garden, lakes and ponds, but the numerous amenities which make the Retiro such a prize attraction. Children make a beeline for the puppet theatre (Sunday performances start at 1pm), while adults may prefer the concerts at the bandstand. There are rowing boats for hire on the lake. Sunday, when there is almost a carnival atmosphere, is the best day to enjoy everything from circus acts and buskers to pavement artists and fortune tellers.

Entertainers dressed as children's characters

🍴 **Refreshment kiosks can be found at various points in the park.**

🎪 **In June a major book fair takes place in the park and is well attended, especially by parents with children.**

- Puerta de Alcalá
- Map G4
- Open Apr–Oct: 6am–midnight; Nov–Mar: 6am–10pm daily
- Dis. access
- Free

Top 10 Features

1. Puerta de la Independencia
2. Estanque
3. Monument to Alfonso XII
4. Paseo de las Estatuas
5. Casita del Pescador
6. Palacio de Velázquez
7. Fuente de la Alcachofa
8. Palacio de Cristal
9. El Ángel Caído
10. Rosaleda

1 Puerta de la Independencia

The handsome Independence Gate *(below)* does not rightfully belong here. It was designed by Antonio López Aguado as the entrance to a palace built by Fernando VII for his second wife, Isabel de Bragança. It is, however, the most important of the park's 18 gates.

2 Estanque

The boating lake *(above)* is one of the oldest features of the park (1631). In the days of Felipe IV it was the setting for mock naval battles. Rowing boats are available for hire from the jetty. Once in a while the lake is drained for cleaning and 6,000 fish have to find a temporary home.

3 Monument to Alfonso XII

This huge monument was conceived in 1898 as a defiant response to Spain's humiliating defeat in Cuba, but the plans were not realized until 1922. The statue of the king is by Mariano Benlliure. The most impressive feature is the colonnade, a popular spot with sun-worshippers.

For more Madrid parks and gardens **See pp50–51**

Paseo de las Estatuas 4

This line of Baroque statues *(right)*, representing the kings and queens of Spain, other Iberian rulers and Aztec chief, Montezuma, was intended to impress.

Plan of the Parque del Retiro

El Ángel Caído 9

This beguiling sculpture, the work of Ricardo Bellver, is said to be the only public monument to the "fallen angel" (Lucifer) in the world. It was unveiled in 1878.

Rosaleda 10

The rose garden holds more than 4,000 roses representing 100 different varieties. Designed by the city's head gardener, Cecilio Rodríguez, in 1915, it is modelled on the Bagatelle in the Bois de Boulogne, Paris.

The Buen Retiro Palace

The park's full title, Parque del Buen Retiro, is a reference to the palace, built for Felipe IV in 1630–32 near the Jerónimos Monastery – *retiro* means retreat. The former royal residence was vandalized by French troops who occupied it during the War of Independence, and eventually demolished. The only parts to survive – the ballroom and the Salón de Reinos – have been earmarked as annexes of the Prado *(see pp12–17).*

Casita del Pescador 5

The "fisherman's house", a typical 18th-century *capricho* (folly), was a part of the re-landscaping of the park in the 1820s. A waterwheel, concealed by the grotto and artificial hill, creates a cascade.

Palacio de Velázquez 6

The Retiro's exhibition centre is the work of Ricardo Velázquez Bosco. The tiled frieze nicely offsets the pink and yellow brick banding.

Fuente de la Alcachofa 7

The "artichoke fountain" *(below)* was designed by Ventura Rodríguez, and made of Sierra de Guadarrama granite and Colmenar stone. The artichoke at the top is supported by four cherubs.

Palacio de Cristal 8

Mirrored in a lake and framed by trees, the Crystal Palace *(left)* was inspired by its British namesake in 1887.

Madrid's Top 10

33

Museo de América

Often overlooked by visitors, this is one of Madrid's best museums. The collection comprises more than 25,000 items recovered from the Americas, including textiles, ceramics, tools, paintings and sculptures. The star of the show, by general consent, is the fabulous Quimbayas treasure, presented to the museum by the Colombian government in the 19th century. The exhibition is organized in five themed areas: how America was perceived in Europe from the Age of the Discoveries to the 18th century; the reality; the evolution of the native societies; religion; and communication between the nations.

Façade

🔵 The museum café is in the basement, but take your drinks to the tables on the first floor where there are views of the grounds.

- Avenida Reyes Católicos 6
- Metro Moncloa
- 91 54 92641
- http://museode america.mcu.es
- Open 9:30am–6:30pm Mon–Sat, 10am–3pm Sun & public hols; closed: 1 Jan, 1 May, 9 Nov, 24 Dec, 25 Dec, 31 Dec
- Dis. access • Adm €3, €1.50 (concessions)

Top 10 Exhibits

1. Caciques Statue
2. Mayan Funerary Urn
3. Jibaro Headdress
4. Huipil
5. Paracas Mummy
6. Shaman Mask
7. Axe
8. Tlingit Helmet
9. Jibaro's House
10. Tro-Cortesian Codex

2 Mayan Funerary Urn
This painted baked-clay urn (cabinet 2.25) dates from AD 600–900, the zenith of the Mayan civilization of Central America. The face on the lid *(below)* represents the deceased.

1 Caciques Statue
Forged in Colombia more than 1,000 years ago, this superb statuette *(below)* in area 4 (cabinet 4.23) is part of the Quimbayas treasure. The fabulous array of gold objects includes earrings, crowns and musical instruments.

3 Jibaro Headdress
This stunning feather headdress (area 1) belongs to the Karajá Indians of Brazil and would have been worn during a ritual dance or other ceremonial. The Karajá are known for their artisanal flair. Less than 500-strong, sadly this small tribe is now under threat.

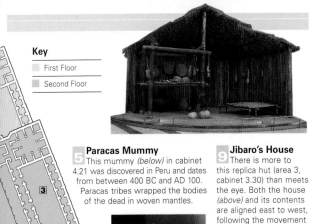

Key

First Floor

Second Floor

Entrance

5 Paracas Mummy

This mummy *(below)* in cabinet 4.21 was discovered in Peru and dates from between 400 BC and AD 100. Paracas tribes wrapped the bodies of the dead in woven mantles.

9 Jibaro's House

There is more to this replica hut (area 3, cabinet 3.30) than meets the eye. Both the house *(above)* and its contents are aligned east to west, following the movement of the sun. The hut itself represents the cosmos while the roof beam represents the union of heaven and earth.

10 Tro-Cortesian Codex

One of only four Mayan manuscripts in existence, the Tro-Cortesian Codex's heiroglyphs depict ancient rituals and divinatory formulae used by priests to depict the future. The 112-page codex is the work of a single scribe.

6 Shaman Mask

This beautiful mask in area 4 (cabinet 4.8) belongs to the Tapirapé Indians of Brazil. The Tapirapé believed that only the shaman could protect them from malevolent spirits.

4 Huípil

A *huípil* (pronounced wee-peel) is an embroidered tunic, and this one *(below)*, in area 3 (cabinet 3.9), is from Guatemala and is decorated with fertility motifs. The design designates the wearer's village, social and marital status, wealth, religious beliefs and much else besides. A woman might own two or three *huípils* during her life.

7 Axe

Inca craftsmen fashioned this ceremonial axe (area 3, cabinet 3.92) from bronze, then encrusted it with copper and silver. The Inca empire flourished between AD 1200 and 1530. The axe was a symbol of imperial power.

8 Tlingit Helmet

This colourful helmet in area 3 (cabinet 3.39) was made from wood, copper, leather and shells by Tlingit Indians of south Alaska.

Museum Guide

The entrance is on the ground floor where visitors will also find the toilets, cloakrooms and a small museum bookshop. The reception area also leads to the Temporary Exhibitions room. Plans of the museum are available at the ticket counter. A broad staircase leads to the first floor and the beginning of the permanent exhibition. From here, signs point visitors in the right direction for a thematic tour of the displays. Area 3 continues on the second floor.

🔟 El Escorial

Enjoying a suitably majestic setting in the southern foothills of the Sierra de Guadarrama, the Royal Monastery of San Lorenzo de El Escorial was commissioned by Felipe II as a mausoleum for the tomb of his father, Carlos I. The name commemorates the victory over the French at St Quentin on the Feast of St Laurence, in 1557. Building began in 1563 and, from the outset, the king took a keen interest in the smallest details of the project, even down to the choice of site. The complex was finally completed in 1595 and comprised a basilica, a royal palace, a monastery, a seminary and a library. This stupendous granite monument to the king's personal aspirations and to the ideals of the Catholic Counter-Reformation still inspires awe, if not always affection.

View of El Escorial

🍴 San Lorenzo del Escorial has a good selection of bars and restaurants.

⏰ Queues build up after midday and on Wed and Thu 5–8pm Apr–Sep and 3–6pm Oct–Mar when admission is free.

• Calle de Juan de Borbón y Battenberg
• Train C-8 from Atocha or Chamartín to El Escorial, then bus from train station to San Lorenzo de El Escorial; buses 661 & 664 from Moncloa to San Lorenzo El Escorial
• 91 890 5904
• www.patrimonio nacional.es
• Open Apr–Sep: 10am–8pm Tue–Sun; Oct–Mar: 10am–6pm Tue–Sun; closed 2 May, 11 Sep
• Adm €10, €5 (concessions), €7 + ticket price (for a guided tour)
• To visit the Bourbons rooms (Aposentos de los Borbones), you will need to book in advance Adm €3.60

Top 10 Features

1. Basílica
2. King's Apartments
3. Pantheon of the Kings
4. Chapter Houses
5. Library
6. Gallery of Battles
7. Main Staircase
8. Strolling Gallery
9. Courtyard of the Kings
10. Architecture Museum

1 Basílica
The basílica *(above)* takes the form of a Greek cross, with vaults decorated with frescoes by Luca Giordano.

2 King's Apartments
Felipe II's personal quarters appear surprisingly modest – just three simply furnished rooms with whitewashed walls and terracotta tiling. Look out for the hand chair used to carry the gout-ridden king on his last journey here in 1598.

3 Pantheon of the Kings
Work on the domed burial chamber *(left)*, directly under the high altar of the basílica, was completed in 1654. The walls were surfaced with marble, bronze and jasper by Giovanni Battista Crescenzi.

Chapter Houses
The vaulted ceilings *(above)* were decorated in the 17th century by Italian artists Fabrizio Castello and Nicola Granelo. Hanging from the walls are priceless canvases by Titian, Tintoretto, Veronese, Velázquez and El Greco.

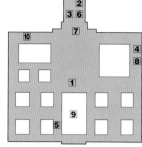

Plan of El Escorial

Courtyard of the Kings
This courtyard *(left)* offers the best view of the basílica façade, its twin belltowers and awe-inspiring dome. The larger-than-life statues of Old Testament kings over the portal give the courtyard its name.

Architecture Museum
This small exhibition of plans, scale models and workmen's tools explains how El Escorial was constructed. Note the wooden cranes and hoists used to haul the blocks of granite into place.

Library
The magnificent barrel-vaulted hall has stunning ceiling frescoes by Italian artists *(above)*. The shelves contain 4,000 precious manuscripts and 40,000 folio volumes – arranged facing outwards to allow air to permeate the pages.

Gallery of Battles
This gallery is decorated with superb frescoes by 16th-century Italian artists. The paintings were intended to validate Felipe II's military campaigns.

Main Staircase
Look up from this magnificent staircase to admire the "Glory of the Spanish monarchy" frescoes by Luca Giordano.

Strolling Gallery
Felipe II enjoyed indoor walks in this airy gallery. The meridians on the floor were added in the 18th century.

Felipe II's Vision

Before architect Juán Bautista de Toledo was allowed to embark on El Escorial, Felipe gave him precise instructions. He should aim for "simplicity in the construction, severity in the whole, nobility without arrogance, majesty without ostentation." When Toledo died in 1577, his successor, Juan de Herrera, followed Felipe's precepts. The design was intended to resemble the iron grid on which St Laurence was roasted alive.

Left **Cenotaphs** Right **King's Deathbed**

Further Features of El Escorial

1 Cenotaphs
These superb bronze sculptures on either side of the high altar are by an Italian father and son team, Leone and Pompeo Leoni. On the left is Carlos I (Emperor Charles V), shown with his wife, daughter and sisters; opposite is Felipe II, three of his wives and his son, Don Carlos.

2 King's Deathbed
It was in this simple canopied bed that Felipe II died on 13 September 1598, it is said as "the seminary children were singing the dawn mass". The bed was positioned so that the king could easily see the high altar of the basilica on one side and the mountains of the Sierra de Guadarrama on the other.

The Martyrdom of St Maurice and the Theban Legion, El Greco

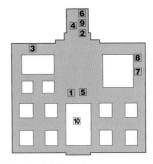

El Escorial Floorplan

3 The Martyrdom of St Maurice and the Theban Legion
This ethereal work by El Greco (1541–1614) was intended for an altar in the basilica but Felipe II found the style inappropriate and relegated it to the sacristy. El Greco never received another royal commission.

4 Portrait of Felipe II
In this stately painting by Dutch artist Antonio Moro, the king, then aged 37, is wearing the suit of armour he wore at the battle of St Quentin in 1557. It was to be Felipe's only victory on the battlefield.

5 Cellini Crucifix
Florentine master craftsman Benvenuto Cellini sculpted this exquisite image of Christ from a single block of Carrara marble. It was presented to Felipe II in 1562 by Francisco de Medici, Grand Duke of Tuscany.

Calvary
6 This moving painting is by 15th-century Flemish artist Rogier van der Weyden. Felipe II knew the Netherlands well and was an avid collector of Flemish art.

Calvary

Last Supper
7 Venetian artist Titian undertook numerous commissions for El Escorial. Unfortunately this canvas was too big to fit the space assigned to it in the monks' refectory and was literally cut down to size.

Inlay Doors
8 One of the most striking features of the king's apartments is the superb marquetry of the inlay doors. Made by German craftsmen in the 16th century, they were a gift from Emperor Maximilian II.

King's Treasures
9 A cupboard in the royal bedchamber contains more than a dozen priceless *objets d'art*. They include a 12th-century chest made in Limoges and a 16th-century "peace plate" by Spanish craftsman Luís de Castillo.

Queen's Room Organ
10 The corridors of El Escorial would have resounded to monastic plainchant but the organ also met with royal approval. This rare hand organ dates from the 16th century and is decorated with Felipe II's coat of arms.

Top 10 El Escorial Statistics
1. 2,673 windows
2. 1,200 doors
3. 300 monastic cells
4. 88 fountains
5. 86 stairways
6. 73 statues
7. 42 chapels (basilica)
8. 16 courtyards
9. 14 entrance halls
10. 80,000 visitors a year

Portrait of Felipe II
Venetian artist Titian completed this portrait of the king in 1551. It now hangs in the Museo del Prado (see pp12–15).

King Felipe II

When Felipe II took over the reins of government from his father Carlos I in 1556, he inherited not only the Spanish kingdoms of Castile and Aragon, Naples, Sicily, Milan and the Low Countries, but also the territories of the New World. Defending this far-flung empire embroiled him in constant warfare. The drain on the royal coffers (despite the prodigious influx of gold and silver from the Americas) led to unpopular tax increases at home and eventual bankruptcy Felipe's enemies, the Protestant Dutch, their English allies and the Huguenot French, set out to blacken his reputation, portraying him as a cold and bloodthirsty tyrant. Today's historians take a more objective view, revealing him to have been a conscientious, if rather remote, ruler and a model family man with a wry sense of humour. On one occasion he startled the monks of El Escorial by encouraging an Indian elephant to roam the cloisters and invade the monastic Cells.

Left **Plaza Mayor in the Golden Age** Right **Madrid during the Civil War**

Moments in History

1 Birth of a City
The first inhabitants of Madrid were Muslim soldiers under the command of Muhammad I. The founding of the city is usually dated to AD 852 when a fortress *(alcázar)* was built on the escarpment now occupied by the Palacio Real *(see pp8–11).* Few traces of this early settlement survive, apart from a small section of the city wall *(see p108).*

2 Christian Conquest
Muhammad I had built his fortress to guard against attack from northern Christian armies and to protect the important city of Toledo. In 1083 Toledo fell and the *alcázar* of Madrid was surrendered without a fight. The new Christian settlers lived harmoniously with their Arab neighbours (although mosques were converted into churches).

3 New Capital
In 1561 Felipe II took the decision to make Madrid his new capital (previously Valladolid had been preferred). The central location and proximity to other royal residences were determining factors. Madrid was still a small, squalid town of 9,000 inhabitants – one of the king's first decisions was to transform the old marketplace outside the walls into a public square, now Plaza Mayor *(see pp18–19).*

Carlos III

4 Golden Age
By the time the Plaza Mayor was completed (1619) Madrid's population had swollen to around 85,000. Courtiers, noblemen, clerics, and criminals descended on the city, leading to such overcrowding that Felipe IV ordered the building of a new perimeter wall. Madrid provided rich material for the playwrights of Spain's Golden Age including Lope de Vega and Tirso de Molina.

5 Mayor-King
Madrid thrived during the reign of Carlos III (1759–88). He gave the city magnificent gateways such as the Puerta de Alcalá *(see p76)* and imposing thoroughfares such as the Paseo del Prado *(see p72–7).* Streets were paved and lit, sewers were dug and nightwatchmen introduced. He became known as *El Rey-Alcalde* (the Mayor-King).

Procession for Carlos III

6 Insurrection

On 2 May 1808, two months after a French army occupied the city, the people of Madrid rose in revolt. Fierce street battles were fought, while the troops of the Monteléon barracks mutinied in support of the rebels. But within a few hours, the insurrection had been crushed and the leaders were executed by firing squad.

7 Re-Awakening

In 1919 Alfonso XIII opened Madrid's first metro line and the city was – literally – on the move again, after decades of inertia. Whole streets were demolished to make way for the Gran Vía's bars and restaurants and Calle de Alcalá became the heart of a new financial district.

8 Madrid Under Siege

Three months into the Spanish Civil War General Franco's Nationalist army surrounded Madrid. Republican resistance was fierce and the siege dragged on for two-and-a-half years, the city finally falling to the rebels in March 1939.

9 Death of Franco

After ruling Spain with an iron fist for 36 years, General Franco died in November 1975, leaving power in the hands of his designated successor, Prince (later King) Juan Carlos. The first democratic elections were held in June 1977.

10 Tejero's Coup

On 23 February 1981 Franco loyalists under Colonel Antonio Tejero attempted a coup. Tejero forced his way into the parliament building, firing shots into the air. The conspiracy collapsed when the king confirmed that the army had remained loyal.

Top 10 Figures in Madrid History

1 Al Mundhir
According to some historians, Muhammed I's son was the true founder the city.

2 Isidro Merlo y Quintana
This devout farm labourer inspired miracles after his death in 1172 and became the city's patron saint (San Isidro).

3 Felipe II
When in Madrid the king stayed in the Alcázar or with the monks of San Jerónimo monastery.

4 Félix Lope de Vega
Spain's greatest playwright was banned from Madrid for eight years after libelling the father of his former lover.

5 Carlos III
Madrid's "best mayor" spent little of the first part of his reign in the city, but his long-term impact is undeniable.

6 Luis Daoíz
With Pedro Velarde, Daoíz led the insurrection against the French in 1808 and died in the fighting.

7 Joseph Bonaparte
Detested during his short reign as King of Spain (1808–12), he did plan one of the city's finest squares, Plaza de Oriente *(see p99)*.

8 Gustavo Durán
One of the most courageous commanders defending Madrid during the Civil War.

9 Francisco Franco
Statues around the city that once honoured the former dictator have all been removed.

10 Enrique Tierno Galván
Madrid's most popular mayor (elected 1979) embraced the *movida (see pp42–3)*.

Left **Pedro Almodóvar** Right **Ouka-Lele**

🔟 People and Places of La Movida

1 Plaza Dos de Mayo
On 2 May 1976 a young couple climbed on to the statue of Daoíz and Velarde and performed a striptease in front of a boisterous crowd of youngsters celebrating on the square. This was one of the first manifestations of the *movida* (scene), a period of hedonism, enthusiasm and creative energy.

2 Pedro Almodóvar
The controversial Academy Award-winning film director shot his first movie, *Pepi, Luci, Bom* in 1980. Iconoclastic and subversive, his bizarre characters – drug-pushing nuns, pill-popping housewives and outrageous transvestites – shocked a society that was only just emerging from the Franco era and captured the spirit of the *movida* on celluloid.

3 Ceesepe
This self-taught artist (real name Carlos Sánchez Pérez) was a leading figure of the *movida*. He produced posters for several of Almodóvar's films, as well as book illustrations, cartoons and record covers. His exhibition, the "Last Supper", in the Moriarty Gallery in 1983, brought him to the attention of a wider public.

4 Ouka-Lele
Madrid-born photographer Ouka-Lele (real name Bárbara Allende) got her big break in 1984 when her work was shown at the Moriarty Gallery. She is now one of Spain's most famous photographers.

5 Moriarty Gallery
Lola Moriarty's art gallery in Calle Almirante (still going strong) was enormously influential in promoting the careers of artists and photographers of the *movida*. Her husband, Borja Casani, was editor of *Luna*, a monthly magazine which published stories by Almodóvar and others. In 1984 Casani hired the entire Hotel Palace for a party attended by several thousand *movidistas*.

6 Mecano
One of Spain's best known pop bands of the *movida* was formed by brothers José and Nacho Cano, and singer Ana Torroja. They hit the big time after persuading a Madrid radio station to play their first single.

Women on the Verge of a Nervous Breakdown, Almodóvar

Mecano

Rock Ola

This La Latina nightclub was one of the most important venues of the *movida* period. Regularly closed down by the police because of drug dealing, it was here that all the influential *movida* bands played.

Enrique Tierno Galván

This former Professor of Marxist philosophy was elected Mayor of Madrid in 1979 and it was his tolerant and relaxed approach that made the *movida* possible. One million people attended his funeral in 1986.

Fashion Designers

The *movida* spawned a new generation of fashion designers who were all to become international names. Jesús del Pozo, Adolfo Domínguez and Ágatha Ruíz de la Prada all flouted the fashion conventions of the day.

Luís Antonio de Villena

Villena's novel *Madrid ha muerto (Madrid has died)*, published in 1999, points out the scene's darker side, as youthful hopes and ideals give way to disillusionment.

Top 10 Moments of La Movida

1 Death of General Franco
The dictator's death in 1975 marked the end of more than 35 years of authoritarian rule.

2 Striptease
This impromptu act in 1976 on Plaza Dos de Mayo reflected a new rebellious spirit in the capital.

3 Enrique Tierno Galván
The liberal-minded mayor was elected in 1979.

4 Pedro Almodóvar
The film director released his first full-length film, *Pepi, Luci, Bom, y otras chicas de Montón* in 1980.

5 Ágatha Ruíz de la Prada
The innovative fashion designer showed her collection in Madrid in 1981.

6 Luna
In 1982 this flagship magazine of the *movida* first appeared, and the city held its first carnival since Franco.

7 El Travelling
In 1983 this bar opened on Calle del Olivar and joined Rock Ola and El Sol as an important *movida* venue.

8 Ouka-Lele
The photographer staged her first show at the Moriarty Gallery in 1984.

9 Law of Desire
Almodóvar's 1986 film explored obsessive homosexual love and starred the young actor Antonio Banderas. It is Spain's top-grossing film.

10 End of La Movida
In 1991 the socialists lost power in Madrid, a sign that the social climate was turning against the *movida*.

Left **Museo Reina Sofía** Right **Museo del Prado**

Museums and Galleries

Museo del Prado
The world-famous gallery is housed in Juan de Villanueva's Neo-Classical masterpiece – an artistic monument in its own right. The relief over the Velázquez Portal depicts Fernando VII as guardian of the arts and sciences – it was during his reign that the Prado opened as an art gallery. Its strongest collection, unsurprisingly, is its Spanish artworks, particularly those of Francisco de Goya (see pp12–17).

Museo Thyssen-Bornemisza
The setting for this outstanding collection is the Palacio de Villa-hermosa, remodelled in the 1990s. Carmen Thyssen-Bornemisza, widow of the preceding baron, was responsible for the salmon-pink colour scheme inside. The museum covers international art from the 14th century onwards (see pp24–7).

Museo Reina Sofía

Museo Reina Sofía
This treasure-house of modern Spanish art was designed as a hospital by Francisco Sabatini in 1756. The conversion to art gallery was completed in 1990. The glass elevators offer panoramic views (see pp28–31).

Museo de América
While the fabled treasures shipped back to Spain by Cortés, Columbus and Pizarro were exhibited as early as 1519, most of the items disappeared or were melted down. These fascinating ethnological and ethnographical exhibits originate from Carlos III's "cabinet of natural history", founded in the 18th century, and now embrace the entire American continent (see pp34–5).

Museo Cerralbo
This astonishingly diverse collection – paintings, sculptures, tapestries, glassware, porcelain and more – were originally the property of the 17th Marquis of Cerralbo. The museum's 30,000 artifacts are housed in his palace and the rooms offer a fascinating window onto the life of Spanish aristocracy at the beginning of the 20th century (see p97).

Museo Arqueológico Nacional
Founded by Queen Isabel II in 1867, the archaeological museum contains treasures from most of the world's ancient civilizations with an emphasis on the Iberian

Peninsula. Highlights include the carved sculpture, the "Lady of Elche", a noblewoman from the 4th century BC *(see p79)*.

Real Academia de Bellas Artes de San Fernando

The Academy of Fine Arts was founded by Fernando VI in 1752 and moved into the Goyeneche Palace 25 years later. Among the highlights are works by Spanish artists El Greco, Velázquez, Murillo, Zurbarán and Goya, as well as an array of European masterpieces *(see p87)*.

Casa-Museo de Lope de Vega

Spain's greatest playwright *(see p41)* lived in this house between 1610 and 1635. Now an evocative museum, the rooms are furnished in the style of the period, based on an inventory made by the dramatist himself *(see p104)*.

Casa-Museo Sorolla

The home of Valencian artist Joaquín Sorolla (1863–1923) is now a delightful museum displaying his work. Sorolla won

Museo Arqueológico Nacional

international recognition after his paintings were exhibited in the Exposition Universelle in Paris (1901). His impressionistic canvases are brilliant evocations of Spanish life *(see p81)*.

Museo Nacional de Artes Decorativas

One of the many pluses of the Decorative Arts Museum is that it sets Spanish crafts in a European context. Highlights include the Gothic bedroom, Flemish tapestries and a collection of 19th-century fans *(see p75)*.

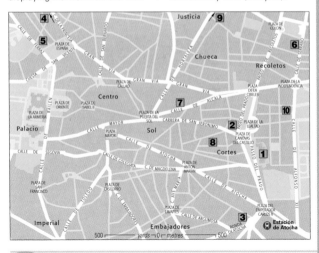

Left **Plaza Mayor** Right **Palacio Real**

Architectural Sights

1 Palacio Real

The Royal Palace marks a decisive break with the austere tastes of Spain's Habsburg rulers. Felipe V had been brought up at Versailles where the International Baroque style was in vogue. Architect Filippo Juvara died two years into the project, but his successor, Gian Battista Sachetti retained the Baroque spirit *(see pp8–12)*.

2 Plaza Mayor

The inspiration for the square was El Escorial's courtyard *(see pp36–9)*. But the plans of architect Juan de Herrera were only realized 30 years in 1619 later by Gómez de Mora *(see pp18–19)*.

3 Palacio de Comunicaciones

Home of the Madrid Town Hall from 2007, this extraordinary building was the first major commission of Galician architect Antonio Palacios and his partner, Joaquín Otamendi. The style of this palace (1905–19) has influences ranging from Spanish Plateresque to Art Deco. The most striking feature of the interior is the stained-glass roof.

🔊 *Calle Montalban 1*
• *Map F4*

4 Palacio Longoria

Art Nouveau is usually associated with Barcelona rather than Madrid and, in fact, this superb example is by the Catalan architect José Grases Riera. Bold and original in design, take a close look at the florid sculptural detail, the sensuous curves and the balustrade – all typical Art Nouveau features *(see p115)*.

5 Círculo de Bellas Artes

The Fine Arts Club dates from the 1920s and is Antonio Palacios' Art Deco masterpiece. The crowning feature is the statue on the roof, representing the goddess Minerva, patroness of the arts. Pay the one-day membership fee and you can take in the other highlights – the staircase, theatre, ballroom and the Salón de Fiestas, with its painted ceiling *(see p87)*.

Metrópolis cupola

6 Metrópolis

One of Madrid's signature buildings, Metrópolis was designed in 1905 by the French architects Jules and Raymond Février. The high point – literally – of this lovely Neo-Baroque confection is the bronze wreaths garlanding the cupola, which glint in the sunlight *(see p88)*.

Puerta de Europa

7 Iglesia de San Jerónimo el Real

Though much altered over the years, this 16th-century church is an important architectural monument. It has also been a place of refuge for Spanish kings and queens through the ages. The current king, Juan Carlos I, was crowned here in 1975 *(see p76)*.

8 Residencia de Estudiantes

Founded in 1910 as a liberal college, early alumni here included artist Salvador Dalí and poet Federico García Lorca. Designed by Antonio Flórez, the main building was nicknamed "trans-atlantic" by students because the balustrade resembled the rail of an ocean liner. ⚓ *Pabellón Transatlántico, Calle del Pinar 21 • Metro Pinar del Rey • Closed to the public*

9 Torre Picasso

The tower's main claim to fame is that, at 157 m (515 ft), it is the tallest building in Madrid. Opened in 1989, it is the work of Japanese architect Minoru Yamasaki, designer of the ill-fated World Trade Center in New York. ⚓ *Plaza de Pablo Ruíz Picasso, Paseo de la Castellana • Map G1*

10 Puerta de Europa

The "Gateway to Europe" is a modern version of a triumphal arch. Twenty-six storeys high, the leaning towers of glass and metal were completed in 1996. ⚓ *Plaza de Castilla • Metro Plaza de Castilla*

Top 10 Places to See Azulejos Tiles

1 Fatigas del Querer

The interior of this 1920's tavern is decorated with Andalusian tiles and murals. ⚓ *Calle de la Cruz 17 • Map P4*

2 Taberna la Dolores

Tiled mosaics adorn the façade of this *taberna* dating from 1908 *(see p77)*.

3 Viva Madrid

Tiled inside and out; look for the Cibeles fountain on the façade *(see p111)*.

4 Villa Rosa

Fantastic ceramic decor dates from the days when this bar was a flamenco club *(see p111)*.

5 Antigua Huevería and Farmacia Juansé

Two tiled frontages. The pharmacy advertised "inoffensive cigarettes", while the painted hens next door are a clue that this bar was once an egg shop (*huevería*). ⚓ *Calle de S Vicente Ferrer • Map D2*

6 Bodega de Angel Sierra

Stunning tiled façade and interior, dating from the early 20th century *(see p123)*.

7 Almendro 13

Andalusian decor can be found in this typical tapas bar *(see p112)*.

8 La Fontana de Oro

Pretty old café converted into a Guinness pub. ⚓ *Calle de la Victoria 1 • Map P4*

9 La Quinta del Sordo

The tiled façade here features scenes from Goya's paintings. ⚓ *Calle del Sacramento 10 • Map C5*

10 Taberna la Daniela

Ceramic motifs cover the bar and façade of this classic Madrid *taberna (see p84)*.

Left **Casa Mira** Right **Seseña**

🔟 Top 10 Spanish Theme Shops

1 Patrimonio Comunal Olivarero

Spain is the largest producer of olive oil in the world and this representative of a grower's cooperative knows his business. Like wines, you can distinguish different varieties by their colour, flavour and smell, and tastings here are part of the fun (see p121).

2 Seseña

This firm near Sol has been making traditional full-length Spanish capes (capas) since 1901, hand-tailored from the finest wool. Famous clients over the years include Picasso, Rudolph Valentino, Hillary Clinton and Michael Jackson. Needless to say, a made-to-measure cape of this quality does not come cheap. ⊗ Calle de la Cruz 23 • Map P4

3 Mesquida

Religion still plays an important role in Spanish life and Madrid is famous for its shops specializing in devotional objects. Founded more than 40 years ago, this family business furnishes churches and monasteries as far afield as Ireland and Argentina and has made items for the Pope's summer residence outside Rome. The store is a showcase of rosaries, statues, cribs, paintings, icons and communion cups. ⊗ Calle Velázquez 156 • Map J4

4 Manuel González Contreras

One of Spain's most respected guitar workshops was founded in 1882. Clients have ranged from the classical virtuoso Andres Segovia to pop guitarist Mark Knopfler. There's a small museum of instruments dating back to the 19th century, and it's fascinating to see the craftsmen at work (see p100).

El Flamenco Vive

5 El Flamenco Vive

If you've been won over by Flamenco during your stay, now's your chance to look the part. This specialist store has everything – colourful costumes and accessories (fans, flowers, ornamental combs), guitars, books, sheet music, videos, records and CDs. ⊗ Calle Conde de Lemos 7 • Map L4

6 Antigua Casa Talavera

Dating back to the early 20th century, Antigua Casa Talavera sells ceramics that are handmade by Spanish potters. Regional styles are represented from all the major centres of ceramics production in Spain, including the famous blue and yellow designs from Talavera de la Reina. Items include decorative tiles, plates, vases, sangria pitchers and reproductions of museum pieces (see p100).

7 Terra Mundi
Apart from its Galician cooking, this restaurant sells regional produce: *chorizo*, *tetilla* (cream cheese), fish soups, pear compote, strawberry liqueur and wines from the Rias Baixas region. ◈ *Calle Lope de Vega 32 • Map R5*

8 Casa Mira
This old fashioned store has been producing its famous nougat *(turrón)* for more than 150 years. Made without artificial colouring or preservatives, it's the genuine article. ◈ *Carrera de San Jerónimo 30 • Map P4*

9 Bodega Santa Cecilia
This wine cellar is popular not only for its range (more than 4,000 labels), but for the quality and affordability. The owners keep prices down by scouring the countryside for lesser-known vineyards. ◈ *Calle Blasco de Garay 74 • Map C1*

10 Cuenllas
This delicatessen is the place for top-quality cured meats and cheeses. Spanish cheeses include Queso Manchego, made from sheep's milk, and the blue cheese, Cabrales. For the finest cured hams, buy *jamón Ibérico* or *Pata Negra* – a breed of pig fed only on acorns. ◈ *Calle Ferraz 5 • Map B2*

Queso Manchego

Top 10 Markets

1 El Rastro
Madrid's famous flea market takes place every Sunday morning *(see pp22–3)*.

2 Ferias de Artesanía
Craft fairs spring up all over the city the week before Christmas. Try Plaza Mayor or Plaza de las Comendadoras.

3 Mercado de Sellos
Stamp and coin collectors meet Sunday mornings under the arches of Plaza Mayor.

4 Mercado de la Cebada
This food market's origins date back to the 16th century. ◈ *Plaza de la Cebada 15 • Map L6 • Mon–Fri & Sat am*

5 Mercado de las Maravillas
Fresh fruit and vegetables, bread, cured ham and cheese. ◈ *Calle Bravo Murillo 22 • Metro Alvarado • Mon–Fri & Sat am*

6 Mercado de Chamartín
Fish and gourmet products. ◈ *Calle Bolivia 9 • Metro Colombia • Mon–Sat am*

7 Mercado de San Miguel
Delicatessen stalls selling food and drink that can be enjoyed on site *(see p101)*.

8 Mercado de la Paz
The main attraction of this small market is the cheese stalls. ◈ *Calle Ayala 28 • Map G2 • Mon–Sat am*

9 Mercado de San Antón
Flowers, food and wine. ◈ *Calle Augusto Figueroa 24/ Calle Libertad • Map R2 • Mon–Fri*

10 Feria del Libro
Old, new and second hand books. ◈ *Calle de Claudio Mayano • Map F6 • Sun am*

Left **Parque del Retiro** Right **Estación de Atocha**

🔟 Parks and Gardens

1 Parque del Retiro

In 1767, Carlos III broke with tradition by allowing members of the public into the Retiro, providing they were "washed and suitably dressed". However it was not until the 1860s and the advent of the First Republic that the partitions separating the royal enclosure from the public area were finally torn down for good *(see pp32–3)*.

2 Jardín Botánico

The botanical garden is the perfect place to recharge the batteries after the exhausting walk around the Prado Museum. The shady paths are lined with statues, the air cooled by judiciously sited fountains *(see p74)*.

3 Jardines de Campo del Moro

Surprisingly, the gardens in the palace grounds were not laid out until the 19th century. The name, "Moor's field" refers to the Arab general, Ali Ben Yusuf, who is said to have camped here while besieging the city after it had fallen to the Christians. On a fine day, the views of the palace and the Casa de Campo from here are unbeatable *(see pp8–11)*.
✪ *Map A4 • Open Apr–Sep: 10am–8pm Mon–Sat, 9am–8pm Sun; Oct–Mar: 10am–6pm Mon–Sat, 9am–6pm Sun*
• Can close for official ceremonies • Free
• Dis. access

4 Parque del Oeste

This lovely park was designed in the early 20th century by Cecilio Rodríguez, head gardener at the Retiro. Apart from the *rosaleda* (rose garden), the main attraction is the Temple of Debod, an ancient monument dating from the 2nd century BC. It was a gift from the Egyptian government. Cafés abound on Paseo del Pintor Rosales, a terminus of the Teleférico *(see p53)*. ✪ *Paseo Horetz • Map B2 • Free*
• Dis. access • Closed to cars at weekends

5 Casa de Campo

The city's largest green space and Felipe II's favourite hunting ground was opened to the public with the overthrow of the monarchy in 1931. Attractively planted with pines, oaks, poplars, and other trees, there are also huge areas of open space, mostly scrub.

Parque del Retiro

Amenities include cafés, picnic areas, restaurants, a boating lake, a zoo and the Parque de Atracciones amusement park *(see p52)*. ◈ *Carretera de Rodasos (bicycles only)* • *Metro Lago or Casa de Campo* • *Free*

Parque Juan Carlos I

This attractive park lies within the exhibition grounds of the Campo de las Naciones. Highlights include catamaran trips on the river and the largest fountain in Spain, with 300 jets. ◈ *Metro Campo de las Naciones* • *Open Jun–Sep: 7–3am Sun–Thu, 7–1am Fri & Sat; Oct–May: 7am–11pm Sun–Thu, 7am–midnight Fri & Sat* • *Free* • *Dis. access*

Jardines de Sabatini

These small gardens next to the Palacio Real occupy the site of the royal stables. Laid out in the 1930s, the design was based on original 18th-century plans. A quiet, restful place for a picnic *(see pp8–11)*. ◈ *Map J2* • *Open May–Sep: 9am–10pm daily; Oct–Apr: 9am–9pm daily*

Parque de Berlín

When the Berlin Wall came down in 1989, everyone wanted a piece of the action. Set among the fountains at the far end of this park, near the Auditorio Nacional *(see p57)*, are three sections of the wall with original

Parque del Oeste

graffiti. Children's play areas and places to eat and drink are nearby. ◈ *Príncipe de Vergara* • *Metro Concha Espina* • *Free* • *Dis. access*

Estación de Atocha

The space beneath the magnificent iron-and-glass canopy at Madrid's central railway station is occupied by a miniature botanical garden, replete with palms and tropical plants *(see p75)*.

Parque El Capricho

These delightful 18th-century gardens belonged to the palace of the Duke and Duchess of Osuna and were landscaped by Jean-Baptiste Mulot, the gardener at Versailles, outside Paris. They have been restored to their former glory with tree-lined paths, fountains, a lake and follies. ◈ *Paseo de la Alameda de Osuna* • *Metro El Capricho* • *Open 9am–6:30pm Sat, Sun & public hols (to 9pm Apr–Sep)* • *Closed 1 Jan, 25 Dec* • *Free* • *Dis. access*

Jardines de Campo del Moro

Left **Parque de Atracciones** Right **Clown, Parque del Retiro**

🔟 Children's Attractions

1 Zoo-Aquarium

Madrid zoo, is considered one of the best in Europe – within its confines there are over 2,000 animals from 500 species, including the endangered white tiger. Young children, in particular, will enjoy the koalas. Free-flying birds of prey are the main draw of the aviary while sharks and other creatures of the deep lurk in the Aquarium. The Dolphinarium shows are another popular attraction. ◈ *Road A-5, exit (salida) 5 Casa de Campo • Metro Casa de Campo • Opening times vary, consult website: www.zoomadrid.com/calendario • Adm (free under 3 years of age)*

2 Parque de Atracciones

This park boasts more than 40 stomach-churning rides as well as a host of other diversions like puppet and magic shows, and a virtual reality zone. The rides include Los Rápidos (a chance to try white-water rafting) and

Dolphinarium, Zoo-Aquarium

Top Spin, which needs no explanation. For the very young there are merry-go-rounds and train and boat rides. ◈ *Casa de Campo • Road A-5, exit (salida) Parque de Atracciones • Metro Batán • Opening times vary, consult website: www.parque deatracciones.es/horarios • Adm (free for children under 90 cm/35 inches in height)*

3 Faunia

Each of the 10 pavilions in this science park has been designed to recreate a different ecosystem with authentic sights, sounds and smells. Visitors can "experience" a tropical storm, journey to the polar regions and observe nocturnal creatures in their natural habitat. ◈ *Avenida de las Comunidades 28 • Road A-3, exit (salida) 6 Valdebernardo • Metro Valdebernardo • Opening times vary, consult website: www.faunia.es/horarios • Dis. access • Adm (free under 3 years of age)*

4 Warner Brothers Park

This vast site is divided into themed areas: Superheroes is devoted to the fantasy worlds of Gotham City and Metropolis, and The Wild West recalls Hollywood westerns of the John Wayne era. You can also tour the replicated film sets of the Warner Brothers Studio. ◈ *Camino de la Warner, San Martin de la Vega • Road A-4, exit (salida) 22 • Train C-3A from Atocha • Opening times vary, consult website: www.parquewarner.com/calendario • Adm (free for children under 100 cm/ 39 inches in height)*

Throughout the Parque de Atracciones you'll find restaurants, bars and fast food outlets for when the kids get hungry.

5 Xanadú

This snow park combines a skiing area and ski school with a vast shopping centre. Other amenities include cinemas, restaurants, bowling and go-karting. ◈ *Road A-5, exit (salida) 22 Arroyomolinos • Bus 528, 534 or 539 from Príncipe Pío • Shops: open 10am–10pm daily, closed 1 & 6 Jan, 25 Dec; Cinema and Snow Park: open 10am–10pm daily (to 2am Fri–Sun)*

6 CosmoCaixa

This state-of-the-art science museum aims to stimulate and surprise with interactive displays and hands-on gadgetry. Younger children can enjoy the Toca Toca zone where they learn about plants and animals, while the highlight for older children is the planetarium. ◈ *Calle Pintor Velázquez, Alcobendas • Road A-1, exit (salida) 16 Alcobendas • Train C-1 from Atocha • Metro Marques de Valdavina • Open 10am–8pm Tue–Sun • Closed 1 Jan, 6 Jan, 25 Dec • Dis. access • Adm*

7 Aquópolis

On offer at Madrid's water park is a range of giant water slides, toboggans, cascades and spirals. There's also a lake, wave pool and toddlers' paddling pool, as well as cafés and restaurants. ◈ *Road A-2 (15.5km) San Fernando de Henares • Open May & Jun: 12:30–7pm (from noon Sat & pub hols); Jul & Aug: 12:30–8pm (from noon Sat & pub hols); 1 & 2 Sep: noon–7pm • Adm*

8 Tren de la Fresa

Great fun for the kids and a nostalgic journey into the past for the grown-ups, the "Strawberry Train", pulled by an old steam locomotive, follows the original route from Madrid to Aranjuez which first opened in 1850. Hostesses wearing period

Teleférico

costume give out helpings of the strawberries for which Aranjuez is famous. The price of the ticket includes the bus ride from the station, as well as entry to the palace, gardens and other attractions. ◈ *Museo del Ferrocarril: Paseo de las Delicias 61 • Metro Delicias • Map F6 • Depart May, Jun, Sep–mid-Oct: 10am Sat & Sun; Return: 7pm • Adm (free under 4 years of age)*

9 Teleférico

The cable car ride between Parque del Oeste and Casa de Campo is enjoyable for both kids and parents. There are fabulous views of the city skyline – the leaflet will help locate landmarks such as the Telefónica building, Torre Picasso, Torre Madrid and the Palacio Real. ◈ *Paseo del Pintor Rosales • Map A2 • Opening times vary, consult website: www.teleferico.com • Adm (free under 3 years of age)*

10 Parque del Retiro

The Retiro's central location makes it an obvious place to visit if the children are in the mood to run wild. On Sunday afternoons (1pm), take them to the puppet show in the open-air theatre near the lake. They won't need to know Spanish as the sense of fun is infectious *(see pp32–3)*.

Left **Carnival** Right **San Isidro**

⑩ Religious and Cultural Fiestas

1 New Year's Eve
To be among the crowds on the Puerta del Sol on the most exciting night of the year is an unforgettable experience. On the stroke of midnight join the revellers in observing the custom of swallowing grapes, one after each chime. Bags of grapes and bottles of sparkling wine are sold from stalls nearby. ◈ 31 Dec

2 Epiphany
Rounding off the Christmas festivities is the *Cabalgata de Reyes* (procession of the kings). Floats parade along Calle Alcalá, through Puerta del Sol, ending in Plaza Mayor. The three kings are played by local politicians. ◈ 5 Jan

3 Carnival
The fun begins the weekend before Shrove Tuesday with fancy dress competitions, brass bands, and a procession followed by a spectacular show on Plaza Mayor. Ash Wednesday is marked by the "Burial of the Sardine". The mock funeral procession leaves from the church of San Antonio de la Florida and ends with interment in the Casa del Campo. ◈ Feb

4 Holy Week
The three days leading up to Easter are marked by solemn religious processions. On Holy Thursday the image of Jesus is carried through the city by penitents wearing the traditional purple hoods and chains around their feet. The following evening is the procession of Jesús de Medinacelli which leaves from the basílica of the same name before winding its way around the city centre. ◈ Mar/Apr

5 San Isidro
The feast day of Madrid's patron saint is celebrated with a procession to the Ermita de San Isidro. *Madrileños* dress up in traditional costumes and picnic on *rosquillas*. There is also a fair, brass bands and sports events. San Isidro also marks the beginning of the bullfighting season. ◈ 15 May

6 Veranos de la Villa
The Summer Arts Festival is a season of concerts (pop, classical, flamenco), theatre productions, ballets

Carnival

Procession, Holy Week

and films, featuring international as well as Spanish artists. Venues range from major theatre and concert halls to the Centro Cultural Conde Duque *(see p56)*. ◈ *Jul–Sep*

7 Neighbourhood Festivals
Each neighbourhood *(barrio)* organizes its own celebrations to mark local red-letter days. These range from the blessing of pets in the church of San Antón, Calle Hortaleza (17 January) to Chinese New Year in Lavapiés (end of January, early February).

8 Festival de Otoño en Primavera
This major cultural festival promotes the arts with an ambitious programme of dance music, drama and film. Events are held in venues across the city. ◈ *early May–early Jun*

9 Virgen de la Almudena
On the Feast of the Virgin of Almudena, the image of the patroness of Madrid is carried in procession through the centre of the city, followed by mass in the cathedral which bears her name *(see p98)*. ◈ *9 Nov*

10 Christmas Crib Fair
The large Christmas Fair on Plaza Major has more than 100 booths, selling cribs *(belenes)*, crib figures, trees and decorations. ◈ *1 Dec–8 Jan*

Top 10 Celebratory Cakes

1 Roscón de Reyes
Circular brioches flavoured with almonds and candied fruit. Usually contain a small charm. ◈ *6 Jan*

2 Panecillos de San Antonio
These small rolls marked with a cross are served at the Church of San Antonio. ◈ *13 Jun*

3 Torrijas
These are slices of milk-soaked bread which have been fried and laced with cinnamon and sugar. ◈ *Holy Week*

4 Monas de Pascua
Very sweet brioches which are, rather strangely, eaten with hard-boiled eggs. ◈ *Holy Week*

5 Rosquillas del santo
Small doughnuts with a variety of flavours and bizarre names – "the fool", "the intelligent one" and "Santa Clara" are just some of them. ◈ *15 May*

6 Suspiros de modistillas
"Needlewomen's sighs" are meringues filled with praline. ◈ *13 Jun*

7 Huesos de santo
Marzipan sweets sculpted to look like "saints' bones". ◈ *1 Nov*

8 Buñuelos de viento
Small profiteroles filled with cream, custard or chocolate. ◈ *1 Nov*

9 Turrón
Nougat, hard or soft, and made in various flavours. ◈ *Christmas*

10 Polvorones
"Crumbly" biscuits flavoured with cinnamon and almonds. ◈ *Christmas*

Left **Centro Cultural Conde Duque** Right **Auditorio Nacional de Música**

Entertainment Venues

1 Centro Cultural Conde Duque

For most of the year this cultural centre hosts temporary art exhibitions. During the annual Summer Arts Festival, however, opera, plays and concerts are also on the programme, many of the events staged outdoors.
◈ Calle del Conde Duque 11 • Map C2

2 Cine Doré

This beautiful 1920s cinema is now the headquarters of the National Film Institute. There are two screens showing an excellent selection of classic and contemporary films in the original version and at very reasonable prices. During the summer, films are also shown on an outdoor screen on the terrace (book ahead). The café in the foyer is a good place to meet up with friends (see p108).

3 Teatro Real

Since its renovation in the 1990s, Madrid's splendid opera house has gone from strength to strength. This is the venue for classical operas, such as Mozart and Verdi, performed by international as well as Spanish companies. The season runs from September to July. If all you want to do is look around, the theatre is open for tours and there's a café in the former ballroom (see p98).

4 Teatro Nacional de la Zarzuela

This beautiful theatre dates from 1856 and was built especially to stage zarzuela, a form of light opera unique to Spain and especially popular in Madrid. After decades of neglect zarzuela is now being revived and the theatre commissions new works from time to time as well as performing classic farces such as The Barber of Lavapiés and The Pharoah's Court. The season runs from September to June. During the summer, the theatre is used for Flamenco, ballet and other cultural events. ◈ Calle de Jovellanos 4 • Map E4

5 Casa de América

The Neo-Baroque Palacio de Linares, an architectural monument in its own right dominating the southern end of the Paseo de Recoletos, is now a cultural centre showcasing Latin American arts, with a regular programme of films, exhibitions and concerts. There is also a good bookshop, a café and the Paradís restaurant (see p77).
◈ Plaza de Cibeles 2 • Map F3

Casa de América

Teatro Fernán Gómez
6 Events at this important arts centre range from temporary art exhibitions to ballet, jazz, dramatic plays, *zarzuela* and experimental theatre. ⊗ *Plaza de Colón 4 • Map G2*

Fundación Juan March
7 Fans of modern art will enjoy the temporary exhibitions here, which are world-class. The foundation also sponsors lunch-time chamber concerts and recitals on weekdays, usually starting around noon (monthly programme available from the centre). While you're here, take a look at some of the modern sculptures in the forecourt such as *Meeting Place* (1975) by Eduardo Chillida *(see p80)*.

Auditorio Nacional de Música
8 This modern concert hall, in a residential district north of the centre, is the home of the National Orchestra of Spain and the major venue for symphony concerts from October to June. The Orchestra of the Comunidad de Madrid also plays here, as well as international ensembles. ⊗ *Calle del Príncipe de Vergara 146 • Metro Cruz del Rayo*

Fundación Juan March

La Riviera
9 If you're interested in hearing pop and rock acts such as Massive Attack, Suede or the Rollins Band, this is where they're most likely to perform while in Madrid. Acoustics and visibility are both good (better than many venues) and fans can cool off in the summer when the roof is drawn back. Also holds discos. ⊗ *Paseo de la Virgen • Map A4 • Metro Puerta del Angel, Príncipe Pío*

Teatro Monumental
10 Designed by Teodoro Anasagasti in 1922, this theatre, renowned for its acoustics, is the home of both the RTVE orchestra and choir (Spain's state radio and television company) as well as the acclaimed Madrid Symphony Orchestra. ⊗ *Calle de Atocha 65 • Map E5*

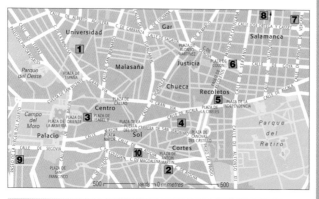

Left **Circuito del Jaráma** Right **Plaza de Toros**

🔟 Sporting Venues

1 Estadio Santiago Bernabéu

The venerated Real Madrid football club celebrated its centenary in 2002, although this 75,000-seater stadium was not completed until 1946. It is named after Santiago Bernabéu, the club president who brought the team five successive European championships in the 1950s. This success has continued – in 1998 FIFA, soccer's world governing body, voted Real Madrid the "best club in the history of football". Their tally to date includes 59 domestic and 15 international trophies, and over five European and nine UEFA champions league cups. Visitors can tour the *sala de trofeos* (trophy room) at the ground. The club also has its own website and television station, broadcasting 20 hours a day. The players are known locally as *merengues* ("meringues") because of their all-white strip. ◑ *Avenida de Concha Espina 1 • Metro Santiago Bernabéu • Trophy room: Open daily except 1 Jan, 25 Dec • Adm (free under 5 years of age)*

2 Estadio Vicente Calderón

Real Madrid's arch-rivals, Atlético de Madrid, play across the River Manzanares in a 55,000-seater stadium, completed in 1966. For most of its history, the club has lived in the shadow of Real Madrid, but all is forgotten when the two clash in annual matches, billed as the "dual of the gods". The club's best season was in 1996 when they brought off a league and cup double, but four years later they suffered the humiliation of being relegated to the second division. The club is due to move to a renovated stadium, Estadio La Peineta, in San Blas in 2014. ◑ *Paseo de la Virgen del Puerto 67 • Metro Pirámides*

3 Palacio de los Deportes

Inaugurated in February 2005, the Palacio de los Deportes (sports palace) occupies the site of a former sports centre that was destroyed by fire in 2001. The building seats 18,000 spectators and was designed to accommodate several sports including athletics, basketball, handball, tennis and boxing. As well as improving safety and security measures the centre's acoustics were improved in order to make it a suitable venue for pop and rock concerts. ◑ *Avenida Filipe II • Metro Goya, O'Donnell*

Estadio Santiago Bernabéu

Club de Campo Villa de Madrid

Plaza de Toros
Bullfighting aficionados are divided over whether it is a sport or an art form. *Corridas* (fights) take place in the Las Ventas stadium (capacity 25,000), which opened in 1931 and even has its own chapel and hospital. Officially the season runs from March to December but the real action begins in May with the Feria de San Isidro (*see p54*). 🔊 *Calle de Alcalá 237 • Metro Ventas*

Jogging Venues
Running isn't much fun in Madrid because of the heavy traffic, although an exception is Paseo Pintor Rosales with views of the Parque del Oeste. Most *madrileños* head for the Retiro, Jardines Sabatini, Casa del Campo or Madrid Rio. Jogging (*el footing*) is popular in the evening when the air is cool.

Outdoor Swimming Pools
Madrid's outdoor swimming pools are open from June to mid-September. There are three pools in the Casa de Campo (children's, intermediate and Olympic), but they are crowded at weekends. An alternative is the Piscina Canal Isabel II. 🔊 *Piscina Canal Isabel II, Avenida de Filipinas 54 • Metro Canal*

El Hipódromo
Horse races are held every Sunday from 11am. Tickets can be booked in advance by phone or in person at the racetrack on Saturdays, 10am–2pm. Visit the stables before racing begins to pick the favourite. 🔊 *Avenida Padre Huidobro, Road A-6, exit (salida) 8 • 91 740 0540 • Closed Dec–Mar*

Madrid Caja Májica
This hi-tech sports complex, designed by architect Dominique Perrault, is dedicated to tennis. It includes 11 indoor and 16 outdoor tennis courts. The site is located close to the Manzanares River, south of the city. 🔊 *Parque Lineal del Manzanares, Calle Camino de Perales • Opening hours vary according to events being held there*

Club de Campo Villa de Madrid
Golf is big business in Spain, thanks to the interest generated by the likes of champions Seve Ballesteros and José Maria Olazábal. Surprisingly, given the generally barren terrain, there are several 18-hole courses in the Greater Madrid area. The Club de Campo was designed by Javier Arana in 1957 and is reckoned to be one of the best in Europe. 🔊 *Carretera de Castilla 2km • Bus Nos. 160, 161 from Moncloa*

Circuito del Jaráma
Fans of motorcar-racing (*automovilísmo*) or motorcycle racing (*motociclísmo*) should head for this 100-acre track, near San Sebastián de los Reyes, 28 km (17 miles) northeast of Madrid. Race meetings are held here throughout the summer. 🔊 *Circuito del Jaráma, Road A-1, 28km • Bus No. 166 from Plaza Castilla*

Left **Joy Madrid** Right **Café Central**

🕙 Nights Out

Casa PATAS
1 If you're interested in flamenco but don't know your *cantadores* from your *bailadores,* this lively club is a good place to get acquainted with the scene. Rated by *madrileños* for its class acts, the show usually starts around 11pm or a little later and continues into the small hours. Beforehand you can have a drink at the bar or order from the range of *tapas,* steaks and plates of fried fish *(see p111).*

Las Carboneras
2 Set to rival Casa PATAS is this Madrid *tablao* (Flamenco club), with its talented and enthusiastic young owners also figuring among the performers. The standard of both resident and visiting acts is excellent, which is why it is making waves among aficionados. Although the show doesn't usually begin until around 11pm, it is advisable to arrive early to be sure of a seat. The club serves typical Spanish snacks. ◎ *Plaza del Conde de Miranda 1 • Map L5*

Café Central
3 Rated as one of the best jazz clubs in Europe, since it first opened in the 1980s it has booked top international acts. The decor – carved wooden ceiling, gilded mirrors, marble tables, maroon seats – is also exceptional. If you get here early, you can while away the time snacking on *tapas (see p111).*

Populart
4 Founded in the early 1990s, this jazz venue, like the Central, is now an important part of the cultural life of the city. The stage is small and space is at a premium, so get here early if you want to see as well as hear the acts – not only traditional jazz, but blues, country, Jazz-Latino, even occasional reggae. Very smoky *(see p111).*

La Negra Tomasa
5 One of the best places in town to hear top salsa bands (and emerging talent) performing live. The show usually starts around 11pm but you'll have to get here much earlier to get a seat. Otherwise you'll join the samba-like queue at the bar, clapping and swaying to the infectious rhythms. Standard Cuban fare served *(see p111).*

Calle54
6 After making the film *Calle54,* Spanish director Fernando Trueba created this club to offer the best in lively latin-jazz. There is also a

Calle54

Casa PATAS

restaurant serving Mediterranean cuisine. The show starts at 11pm and booking is essential. ◉ *Paseo de la Habana 3 • Metro Santiago Bernabeú*

Joy Madrid

Madrid's best-known disco celebrated its 30th anniversary in 2010. Once a 19th-century theatre staging *zarzuela* operettas and music hall, visitors can still gaze down at the dancers from the tiered balconies. A favourite with the city's gilded youth and showbiz crowd, outsiders are more than welcome. Don't bother turning up before midnight – none of the locals will. ◉ *Calle de Arenal 11 • Map M4*

Clamores

This roomy jazz venue also books blues, reggae and gospel acts and, occasionally, Flamenco. The atmosphere is laid back and the audience really gets into the swing of things. Look out for the weekend jam sessions. ◉ *Calle de Alburquerque 14 • Map E1*

Villa Rosa

Villa Rosa has been going for more than 40 years, originally as a Flamenco club, more recently as a disco. Visitors can admire the tiled Andalusian-style interior, shown to good effect in Pedro Almodóvar's Movida-period movie *High Heels*. Very crowded by 1am, more so as the night wears on *(see p111)*.

Palacio de Gaviria

Dance in the footsteps of the Marqués de Gaviria, a 19th-century hedonist who entertained Madrid's high society in this ornate palace near Puerta del Sol. This venue has various bars, each with a different ambience, and there are frequent theme nights. The ballroom is either used for live music, or is colonised by serious dancers getting down to the guest DJs *(see p111)*.

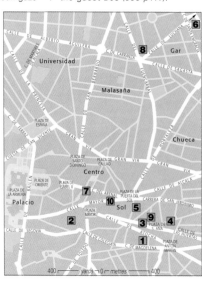

Left **Txangurro** Right **Gazpacho**

Spanish Dishes

Cocido Madrileño
This classic Madrid stew goes back to the days when the working-class housewives of Lavapiés and La Latina *(see p104)* would keep a cooking pot simmering on the stove, adding whatever ingredients came to hand. Today's typical *cocido* might include pigs' trotters, beef shank, chicken, sausage, chickpeas and vegetables. Served in stages, first the broth, then the vegetables and meats, it can be a meal in itself. For an up-market version, try La Bola *(see p101)*.

Cochinillo Asado
The Castilian countryside is famous for its roasts. To be authentic, suckling pig should be cooked slowly in a wood-fired oven until the flesh is tender and the skin golden. Lamb *(cordero)*

Paella

and game such as partridge *(perdiz)* and pheasant *(faisán)* are equally delicious when roasted in the traditional way.

Callos a la Madrileña
Tripe may not be to everyone's taste, but try it "Madrid-style" in a typical *taberna* and you may change your mind. The ingredients of this tasty stew include *chorizo* (Spanish sausage), tomatoes, onions and paprika.

Bacalao
It is said that there are as many ways of cooking this Mediterranean staple of salted cod as there are days in the year. The American writer Ernest Hemingway relished *bacalao al ajoarriero*, a cod stew made with tomatoes, peppers and garlic.

Paella
Sunny Valencia is the acknowledged home of this most famous Spanish rice dish. While traditionally cooked with fish and shellfish, you'll also find meat-based *paellas* (usually rabbit or chicken). The name comes from the two-handled, shallow iron pan in which it is cooked and served.

Pulpo a la Gallega
Octopus "Galician style" originated in a part of the country famous for its fish and seafood dishes. Usually served on a wooden platter, it comes in slices on a layer of potato, with a

62

For the Top 10 tapas dishes **See p67**

large dose of oil and a sprinkling of paprika. *Pulpo a la Gallega* is extremely popular in Madrid.

7 Fabada Asturiana
Asturian farmers swear by this nourishing bean soup as the best way of keeping out the cold. Served piping hot, the other main ingredient is *morcilla* (black pudding). Ideally, wash it down with a glass of Asturian cider.

Fabada Asturiana

8 Txangurro
Spider crab is a Basque delicacy which, purists say, should be served on its own. It is so strongly flavoured that some chefs mix the meat with other seafood before seasoning with parsley and garlic, and returning it to the shell to serve.

9 Merluza Rebozada
Another north country favourite is hake fried in bread-crumbs. This versatile fish is equally tasty cooked in a béchamel (white) sauce made with spicy piquillo peppers, then stuffed into red peppers.

10 Gazpacho
The famous cold soup hails from Andalucia. G*azpacho*'s main ingredients are tomatoes, garlic, cucumber and vinegar, with puréed bread for body.

Top 10 Spanish Wines

1 Rioja
Spain's classiest wines hail from the upper Ebro valley (La Rioja) and have a distinctive, oaky flavour.

2 Rueda
This small, up-and-coming region south of Valladolid produces lively white wines using the Verdejo grape.

3 Rias Baixas
The Albariño grape thrives in cool, wet northwest Spain, known for its fragrant whites – but they don't come cheap.

4 Navarra
Navarra's palatable reds and rosés do not lag far behind those of neighbouring La Rioja, and prices are competitive.

5 Penedès
The Catalonian region has never looked back since Miguel Torres introduced Cabernet Sauvignon and Chardonnay grapes in the 1960s.

6 Jerez
The Andalusian plains just north of Cadiz have been synonymous with sherry production since the 18th century.

7 Ribera del Duero
This region is noted for its high-quality red wines, made with the Tempranillo grape.

8 Valdepeñas
Valdepeñas turns out lightly-flavoured reds with a high alcohol content.

9 La Mancha
Spain's largest wine growing region produces good-value table wines.

10 Cava
A fresh, sparkling wine; the name Cava (cellar) was adopted after the French disallowed use of the word champagne.

Left **Museo Chicote** Right **La Ardosa**

📖10 Bars

1 La Ardosa
This popular watering hole has a pedigree going back more than 200 years – Goya sold some of his paintings here. The pub was given a makeover in the 1980s and the owner claims it was the first bar in Madrid to celebrate St Patrick's night. That was when they started serving Guinness and home-made *tortilla*, one of the mainstays of an enticing *tapas* menu. The subdued lighting, mellow music and amiable clientele create an addictive ambience *(see p123)*.

2 El Parnasillo
Located in the trendy Malasaña district, this café and bar is decorated in *belle époque* style and is one of the oldest cafés in the area. On offer are home-made cakes and a wide choice of coffee. Come early evening for hot drinks or sip one of El Parnasillo's famous cocktails later on. Snacks are also available *(see p122)*.

Cervecería Santa Bárbara

3 Café Manuela
"Manuela" as in Manuela Malasaña *(see p116)*. The statue of the local heroine is a feature of the lovely late 19th-century decor, which includes mirrors, fluted columns and stucco flourishes. The entertainment ranges from concerts and poetry readings (sometimes bilingual) to discussions and exhibitions by local artists. The friendly staff serves coffees, beers or cocktails depending on the time of day, as well as *tapas* *(see p122)*.

4 Ramsés
Swing by the Puerta de Alcalá at 1am and spot Ferraris double parked outside this Philippe Starck designed complex. Popular with Madrid's most fashionable crowd, the large, oval cocktail bar is perfect for people watching, and serves an extensive selection of drinks. There are also two great restaurants and a club in the basement. The delicious weekend brunch is a good hangover cure; choose a table with a view of the plaza *(see p84)*.

5 Museo Chicote
"The best bar in Spain, certainly" was Ernest Hemingway's verdict on this cocktail bar. It was in the 1950s and 1960s, however, that Chicote became really famous, thanks to visiting Hollywood celebrities such as Frank Sinatra. The bar is at its best in the late evening *(see p94)*.

Cervecería Santa Bárbara

A Madrid institution, this large beer hall is the perfect place to unwind after a day's sightseeing or to begin a night on the town. Both dark beer and lager are available on draught – some *madrileños* like to mix the two *(see p123)*.

Cervecería Alemana

This beer and *tapas* bar owes a good deal of its popularity to its terrace on Plaza Santa Ana. Like Museo Chicote, the Alemana was a favourite of Ernest Hemingway and other expats. Spanish and imported beers *(see p108)*.

La Venencia

A bar for sherry drinkers who know their fino from their manzanilla, La Venencia opened its doors in 1929 and still does a roaring trade, especially in the evenings when tourists mingle with a loyal local following. Apart from the decor, which is ageing as graciously as the sherries behind the counter, there's a good selection of canapés and *tapas* such as *mojama* (flakes of salty dried tuna) *(see p112)*.

Alhambra

Designed to look like a bar of the early 1900s with Moorish touches, Alhambra is one of the best places to start the evening if you're about to embark on a tour of the night spots of Sol and Santa Ana. Check out the Andalusian *tapas* – especially the cured meats and spicy

Moore's

sausage. There's also a good selection of Spanish wines available *(see p112)*.

Moore's

Irish bars are incredibly popular with *madrileños*. This one offers all the usual attractions – long opening hours, pub-grub like roast beef, satellite TV coverage of sporting events and good music. Prices are higher than average but the promotions lessen the pain. ✪ *Calle Felipe III 4* • *Map M4*

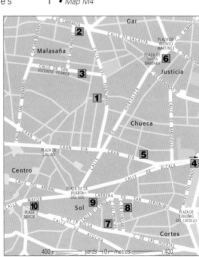

Left **Bodegas Rosell** Right **La Casa del Abuelo**

TOP 10 Tapas Bars

Tasca La Farmacia
Like all genuine Madrid *tascas*, this pub on the edge of Salamanca serves its customers a tasty appetizer with each drink, to give them an idea of what's on offer. *Croquetas de Bacalao* – béchamel paste deep fried with nuggets of cod – are the house speciality *(see p84)*.

Casa Ciriaco
When Ciriaco first opened its doors in 1906, most of the customers were artists, writers and other Bohemian types. Nowadays it's more respectable but Ciriaco has preserved its reputation for excellent *tapas*. The *boquerones* (anchovies in vinegar) go down a treat with a glass of the house wine *(see p101)*.

Los Gatos
Bring your camera when you visit this wonderfully over-the-top bar, often overlooked by tourists. Every inch of space is crammed with bric-à-brac – signed basketball shirts, old telephones, beer barrels, bull's heads, you name it. Steer your way to the bar for a glass of beer and a plate of shrimps. While you're about it, take a look at the tempting array of canapés, filled rolls and delicious *tapas*. ⓢ *Calle Jesús 2* • *Map E5* • *91 429 3067* • *€*

La Casa del Abuelo
Near Plaza Santa Ana, "Grandad's place" is a spit-and-sawdust bar with bags of atmosphere. It's customary to order the house wine to accompany the *tapas* – variations around the humble shrimp. Try them grilled in their shells *(a la plancha)* or peeled and fried in oil and garlic *(al ajillo)*. Standing room only *(see p113)*.

El Bocaíto
The *bocaítos* are small squares of toasted bread, served with a topping of salmon or anchovies. They are the mainstay of an extensive *tapas* menu. Expect quality rather than quantity and keep an eye on how much you're spending, as it's quite easy to run up a fair sized bill *(see p123)*.

La Trucha
This Andalusian-style *tapas* bar has a lovely summer terrace, and is always popular. Sit at the bar and observe *tapas* being prepared in the kitchen, or watch as assorted smoked canapés are made at the cold counter. From the most delicious tortilla in town to deep-fried trout, the choice is outstanding *(see p112)*.

Mixed green olives

Recommend your favourite bar on traveldk.com

7 Bodegas Rosell

Manolo Rosell, the owner of this high-ceilinged *tapas* tavern, has won Spain's "Golden Nose" award for wine-tasting, and proudly serves his discoveries alongside tasty *tapas* (see p77).

8 El Rincón de Goya

Located just off Calle Goya, this is the perfect place to stop and refuel after shopping in Salamanca. The *tapas* are listed on the wall behind the bar, and the most popular are the large, toasted canapés with toppings such as brie, steak, wild mushrooms and prawns. There is a small seating area by the bar (see p84).

Taberna de Antonio Sánchez

9 Taberna de Antonio Sánchez

This Lavapiés hostelry dates from 1830. The wooden furniture and bullfighting memorabilia are as authentic as the menu of tortilla and stews (see p112).

10 Casa Labra

The speciality here is cod croquettes. If you don't fancy standing at the bar, classic Madrid dishes are served in the wood-panelled room at the back (see p94).

Top 10 Tapas Dishes

1 Potato dishes
Including *patatas bravas* (fried, with a spicy tomato sauce) or *patatas alioli* (boiled, with a mayonnaise and garlic dressing).

2 Canapés
The toppings for canapés range from anchovies and egg slices to *morcilla* (black pudding) and smoked salmon.

3 Tortilla
The famous Spanish omelette is far thicker than other cuisines and is made with potatoes. It is often served as an appetizer.

4 Pimientos
Peppers are usually served *rellenos* (stuffed with meat, cod or tuna) or *de padron* – grilled and salted.

5 Empanadillas
These are pastries usually with tuna and tomato or meat fillings.

6 Croquetas
Spanish croquettes are made with a thick béchamel sauce and chopped ham, chicken or cod then deep fried.

7 Raciones
Larger dishes to share, including hot stews, *jamón Serrano* (cured ham), *chorizo* (spicy sausage) or *queso manchego* (sheep's milk cheese).

8 Conservas
Canned fish, including *boquerones* (anchovies) *mejillones* (mussels) and *berberechos* (cockles).

9 Soldaditos de Pavía
These are cod fingers fried in batter.

10 Gambas
Shrimps are grilled in their shells (*a la plancha*) or peeled and then fried in oil and garlic (*al ajillo*).

Left **Viridiana** Right **Isla del Tesoro**

Restaurants

1 Santceloni

This sleek Madrid outpost of renowned Catalan chef Santi Santamaría is one of the city's finest restaurants. The menu features superbly prepared, imaginative dishes. Booking is essential. ◎ *Hotel Hesperia, Paseo de la Castellana 57 • Map G1 • 91 210 8840 • Closed Sat L, Sun, public hols • €€€€€*

2 Botín

On the authority of the *Guinness Book of Records*, Botín is the world's oldest restaurant, having opened its doors in 1725. The dining rooms retain much of their original decor including *azulejo* tiles and oak beams, and the atmosphere is convivial. Botín is famous for Castilian fare and the house speciality, roast suckling pig *(see p113)*.

3 DiverXO

Young chef David Muñoz, who trained at London's Hakkasan and Nobu, was awarded a second Michelin star in 2011 for his exceptional Spanish–Asian fusion cuisine at DiverXO. There are three tasting menus that range from €75 to €120. Try the delectable chile crab. The restaurant seats only 30 people so booking is essential. However, reservations cannot be made more than 30 days in advance. ◎ *Calle Pensamiento 28 • 91 570 0766 • Open Wed–Sun, dinner only • €€€€€*

4 Lhardy

Another Madrid institution, founded in 1839, Lhardy's upstairs dining rooms are wonderfully intimate and more than a touch elegant with *belle époque* gilded mirrors, wainscoting, Limoges china and Bohemian crystal. The cooking is *madrileño* rather than French, the house speciality being *cocido* (chickpea stew) *(see p95)*.

5 Estado Puro

Savour award-winning gastronomic *tapas* at this funky informal establishment run by famed Spanish chef Paco Roncero. The menu incorporates molecular gastronomy and fusion cuisine to create an array of small dishes to mix and match and a medley of sublime flavours. Try the delicious asparagus tempura *(see p94)*.

6 Isla del Tesoro

Madrid has dragged its heels where catering for vegetarians is concerned but one exception is

Estado Puro

"Treasure Island". The owner, Magdalena Madariaga, buys macrobiotic ingredients whenever possible. Try the *nido silvestre* ("wild nest"), a spinach and mushroom salad, topped with parmesan *(see p123)*.

Viridiana

Named after the Buñuel film, this cosy modern *locale* is located between Paseo del Prado and Retiro Park, and is owned by chef Abraham García. This is the perfect restaurant for a special occasion; the menu is imaginative and the wine list is superb *(see p77)*.

La Trainera

Named after the long row boats in the Bay of Biscay, where the restaurant owns a fishing vessel, La Trainera has expanded into a labyrinth of rooms with pine tables and chairs. The menu uses a variety of seafood, not only from the Bay of Biscay but also from Cádiz and the Mediterranean. Try the delicious shellfish salad, *salpicón de mariscos*, and the grilled fish *(see p85)*.

Ramón Freixa Madrid

Ramón Freixa Madrid

Imaginative chef Ramón Freixa blends tradition with innovation in his two-star Michelin restaurant. On offer are three fabulous tasting menus that include everything from turtle dove sausage to stewed snails *(see p85)*.

Asador Arizmendi

What *madrileños* prize here is succulent meat and fish, cooked in the traditional manner over charcoal. If you still have room, try the rice pudding *(arroz con leche) (see p113)*.

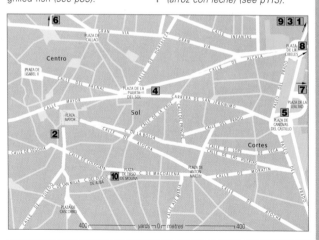

Note: Unless otherwise stated, all restaurants accept credit cards and serve vegetarian meals

AROUND TOWN

MADRID'S TOP 10

Left **Parque del Retiro** Right **Plaza de la Lealtad**

Around Paseo del Prado

THIS IMPOSING TREE-LINED AVENUE, *adorned with fountains and sculptures, is home to no fewer than three world-class art galleries: the Prado, the Reina Sofía and the Thyssen-Bornemisza. In the 18th century the prado was a meadow, crossed by a stream, but the bucolic surroundings were deceptive, as the area was acquiring an unsavoury reputation for muggings and amorous encounters. The solution, devised by Charles IV, was a new boulevard between Plaza de Cibeles and Plaza de Atocha, lined with handsome buildings devoted to the pursuit of scientific inquiry. Work began in 1775 on a museum of natural history (now the Prado), the botanical gardens and observatory and medical school (now the Reina Sofía).*

Estación de Atocha

🔟 Sights

1. Museo del Prado
2. Museo Thyssen-Bornemisza
3. Museo Reina Sofía
4. Parque del Retiro
5. Plaza de Cibeles
6. Plaza de la Lealtad
7. Hotel Ritz
8. Real Jardín Botánico
9. Museo Nacional de Artes Decorativas
10. Estación de Atocha

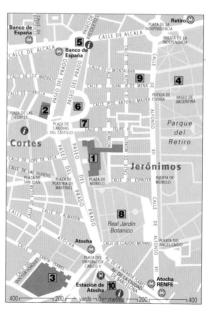

Preceding pages **Monument to Alfonso XII by Estanque, Parque del Retiro**

1 Museo del Prado

One of the world's finest art galleries, the Prado includes a spectacular section of Spanish paintings within its vast collection (see pp12–17).

2 Museo Thyssen-Bornemisza

What began as a private collection is now a superb public museum of some of the best European art from the past 700 years (see pp24–7).

3 Museo Reina Sofía

In contrast to the Prado, this wonderful art gallery is devoted to the very best of 20th- and 21st-century art (see pp28–31).

4 Parque del Retiro

This much-loved city park is a constant source of pleasure to madrileños, especially at weekends and during the hot summer months. There are open spaces to enjoy, as well as wooded areas and formal gardens (see pp32–3).

5 Plaza de Cibeles

One of Madrid's busiest traffic intersections also boasts the city's most famous landmark. The Fountain of Cybele,

Fountain of Cybele, Plaza de Cibeles

designed by Ventura Rodríguez, depicts the goddess of nature and abundance riding her chariot, hauled by a pair of prancing lions. (The water-spouting cherubs were added at the end of the 19th century.) The most striking architectural monument on the square is the over-the-top Palacio de Comunicaciones, now the Madrid Town Hall (see p46). Opposite is the Neo-Baroque Palacio de Linares, one of the city's finest 19th-century buildings, and now the Casa de América (see p56). On the corner of Calle Recoletos, partly hidden from view by its steeply sloping gardens, is the former Palacio de Buenavista, commissioned in 1777 for the Duchess of Alba, a legendary beauty and one-time lover of artist Francisco de Goya. Today it is home to the General Army Barracks. ◊ Map F4

6 Plaza de la Lealtad

This leafy square honours the fallen heroes of the 1808 uprising against the French (see p41). The ashes of the rebel leaders, immortalized in Goya's famous painting (see p13), were interred in the funerary urns beneath the obelisk when the project was finally completed in 1840. The Neo-Classical building occupying the north side of the square is the Madrid Stock Exchange, designed by Enrique María Repullés in 1884. Visitors may admire the Corinthian-columned façade at any time, but anyone wishing to see the trading floor (parquet flooring, painted vaults, stained-glass ceiling and gilded clock) will have to join the guided tour at midday. ◊ Map F4 • Madrid Stock Exchange: Plaza de la Lealtad 1; Tours noon on Thu by appointment (email: exposicion@grupobme.es to book); Free

Hotel Ritz

The Ritz *(see p142)* first opened its doors in 1910 and the inauguration was attended by King Alfonso XIII, who had backed the project after complaining of the lack of quality accommodation in his capital. French architect Charles Mewes' Neo-Classical building is surprisingly understated from the outside, but the interior is predictably opulent. Outstanding features include handwoven carpets from the Royal Tapestry factory and the *belle époque* dining room. Stop for a drink on the terrace. ◐ *Plaza de la Lealtad 5 • Map F4*

Real Jardín Botánico

Anyone seeking a bit of peace and quiet will relish these delightful gardens, inaugurated in 1781 as a centre for botanical research. The three ascending terraces conform to Juan de Villanueva's original design. Beyond the main entrance is the herbarium, the aromatic, culinary and medicinal plants neatly arranged in separate beds and individually labelled. The rose garden adds a dash of colour. The central terrace arranges plants by family, species and genealogical history. Look out for the 100-year-old tree known as *"El Pantalones"* because of its resemblance to a pair of inverted trousers – disease has split the trunk in half. More than 1,200 tropical and sub-tropical species are cultivated in the Exhibition Greenhouse, opened in 1993. The Villanueva Pavilion and the arbors, by contrast, date back to the 18th century. The statue by the pond honours the great Swedish botanist, Carl von Linné (Linnaeus), who devised the system of plant classification. ◐ *Plaza de Murillo 2 • Map F5 • Open 10am–dusk daily • Closed 1 Jan, 25 Dec • Adm*

Museo Nacional de Artes Decorativas

Housed in a 19th-century mansion overlooking the Retiro is this compelling collection of furniture, silverware, ceramics and glassware from the royal factory of La Granja, as well as jewellery, tapestries, clocks, musical instruments and toys. But the museum is more than a showcase of handicrafts. Arranged chronologically over four floors are reconstructed rooms illustrating Spanish domestic life from the 16th to the early 20th centuries. On the

Real Jardín Botánico

Museo Nacional de Artes Decorativas

fourth floor is the recreated Valencian kitchen, decorated with over 1,600 hand-painted *azulejo* tiles. The below-stairs life of an 18th-century palace is vividly brought to life as servants struggle with trays of pies and desserts while the cats filch fish and eels. ✆ Calle de Montalbán 12 • Map G4 • Open 9:30am–3pm Tue–Sat, 5–8pm Thu–Sat, 10am–3pm Sun • Closed 1 Jan, 6 Jan, 1 May, 15 May, 24 Dec, 25 Dec, 31 Dec • Dis. access • Adm

10 Estación de Atocha

Madrid's southern railway station is also a palm garden and an arresting architectural monument. The old terminal, a magnificent cast-iron structure, 152 m (500 ft) long and more than 40 m (130 ft) high, overlooks Plaza de Atocha. It was designed by Alberto del Palacio in 1888 – the French engineer Gustave Eiffel, designer of Paris's famous tower, was a consultant – and completed four years later. When the decision was taken to run a new high-speed train service to Seville (AVE), prize-winning Spanish architect Rafael Moneo was commissioned to remodel the terminal. His makeover incorporated the square and the old station canopy, and added a cylindrical lantern over the commuter station and a streamlined glass concourse from where the AVE now departs. ✆ Glorieta de Carlos V • Map F6 • Dis. access

A Day on the Paseo del Prado

Morning

🕐 Begin at **Plaza de Cibeles** *(see p73)* and take a peek at the palatial central hall of the **Town Hall** *(see p46)*. Plans to redirect traffic away from the Paseo del Prado have been frustrated, but the central boulevard still makes a pleasant walk, with plenty of shade in summer. Cross the road to **Plaza de la Lealtad** and the garden terrace of the **Hotel Ritz** – a delightful spot for coffee. Continue past the Neo-Classical façade of the **Museo del Prado** *(see pp12–17)* and you'll come to Plaza de Murillo and the **Real Jardín Botánico**. Allow at least an hour here to make the most of the verdant tranquillity.

On leaving the garden, cross the Paseo del Prado and double back to Plaza Cánovas del Castillo and Ventura Rodríguez's splendid Neptune Fountain. The small side streets here are crammed with plenty of tempting *tapas* bars and restaurants. You could try **La Platería** for a light lunch *(see p77)*.

Afternoon

After lunch, take the small detour into Plaza de las Cortes, to admire the impressive portico of the **Congreso de los Diputados** *(see p76)*. Return to the Paseo del Prado and on your left is the **Museo Thyssen-Bornemisza** which will occupy the rest of the afternoon *(see pp24–7)*. Take the central boulevard to return to your starting point, Plaza de Cibeles.

Left **Puerta de Alcalá** Right **Museo del Ferrocarril**

Best of the Rest

Puerta de Alcalá
This imposing gateway to the city was designed in 1769 by Francesco Sabatini. ◊ *Map G4*

Real Fábrica de Tapices
The Royal Tapestry Factory was founded in the 18th century. Today's artisans still use the original wooden looms. ◊ *Calle Fuenterrabía 2 • Map H6 • Open 10am–2pm Mon–Fri • Closed 1 Jan, 6 Jan, 1 May, 30 May, Aug, 24 Dec, 25 Dec, 31 Dec • Adm*

Iglesia de San Jerónimo el Real
The Castilian parliament, the Cortes, met in this historic church in 1510. ◊ *Calle Moreto 4 • Map F5 • Open Jul–Sep: 9:30am–1:30pm, 6–8pm Mon–Sat, 9:30am–1:30pm, 5:30–8:30pm Sun; Oct–Jun: 10am–1pm, 5–8:30pm Mon–Sat, 9:30am–2:30pm, 5:30–8:30pm Sun • Free*

Salón de Reinos
The Hall of Kingdoms was part of a 17th century palace. It has now been acquired by the Museo del Prado *(see pp12–17)*. ◊ *Méndez Núñez 1 • Map F4 • Closed until 2015*

Museo Naval
Among the highlights here is a 16th-century Flemish galleon and the first map of the New World. ◊ *Paseo del Prado 5 • Map F4 • Open Sep–Jul: 10am–7pm Tue–Sun • Closed Aug, public hols • Free*

Museo del Ferrocarril
The railway museum has a wonderful collection of old steam locomotives on display and is the departure point for the Tren de la Fresa *(see p53)*. ◊ *Paseo de las Delicías 61 • Map G6 • Open Sep–Jul: 10am–3pm Tue–Sun & Mon over Christmas • Closed 1 Jan, 6 Jan, 1 May, 25 Dec • Adm*

Westin Palace
This has been one of Madrid's most luxurious hotels since it opened in 1913 *(see p142)*.

Plaza de Murillo
The decorative centrepiece of this small square is the Apollo fountain, designed in 1781 by Ventura Rodríguez. ◊ *Map F5*

Observatório Astronómico
The National Observatory museum includes historic telescopes and other astronomical instruments. ◊ *Calle Alfonso XII 3 • Map G6 • Open Fri–Sun (by appointment) • Adm*

Congreso de los Diputados
Admire the portico and Renaissance-style sculptures of the congress building on a guided tour. ◊ *Carrera de San Jerónimo • Map E4 • 91 390 6000 • Open 10:30am–12:30pm Sat • Closed Aug, public hols • Free*

If you want to take a tour of the Congreso de los Diputados, take your passport with you as a form of ID.

Price Categories

For a three-course meal for one with half a bottle of wine (or equivalent meal), taxes and extra charges.

€	under €25
€€	€25–€35
€€€	€35–€55
€€€€	€55–€70
€€€€€	over €70

Above **La Platería**

Top10 Places to Eat

1 Senzone
Acclaimed chef Francisco Morales and his wife, Ruth Controneo, a sommelier, run this wonderful restaurant. Expect inventive, seasonal cuisine. ✆ *Hotel Hospes, Plaza de la Independencia 3 • Map G3 • 91 432 2911 • €€€€*

2 Le Cabrera de Casa de America
Housed in a historic building, this stylish restaurant has a delightful terrace and offers creative cuisine at affordable prices. ✆ *Calle Recoletos 4 • Map F3 • 91 577 5955 • €€*

3 Horcher
One of Madrid's most exclusive restaurants, Horcher specializes in the cooking of central Europe, in particular game. ✆ *Calle de Alfonso XII 6 • Map F4 • 91 522 0731 • Closed Easter, Aug, 24 & 25 Dec • €€€€€*

4 Café del Botánico
Located near the Botanical Gardens, this elegant restaurant serves a good selection of drinks and food. ✆ *Calle Ruiz de Alarcón 27 • Map F5 • 91 420 2342 • €*

5 Café Restaurant Samarkanda
Enjoy Mediterranean cuisine, coffee and cocktails here. ✆ *Glorieta de Carlos V, Atocha Station • Map F6 • 91 530 9746 • €€€*

6 La Taberna la Dolores
This classic *taberna* has kept its original tiled frontage, dating from 1908. The canapés *(pulgas)* are recommended. ✆ *Plaza de Jesús 4 • Map E4 • 91 429 2243 • €€*

7 VIPS
The shop-café *(see p139)* is always busy. Everything from ham and eggs to bowls of tacos is on the menu. Breakfast is served until midday. ✆ *Plaza de Canovas de Castillo 5 • Map E4 • 91 275 2183 • €€*

8 La Platería
Situated off the Paseo del Prado, there's a terrace where you can snack on Castilian dishes such as *jamón Ibérico* and goat's cheese. ✆ *Moratín 49 • Map F5 • 91 429 1722 • €*

9 Viridiana
Master chef Abraham García's bistro offers a sensational menu and wine list. ✆ *Calle Juan de Mena 14 • Map F4 • 91 523 4478 • Closed Sun, Easter, 24 & 25 Dec • €€€€€*

10 Bodegas Rosell
This classic Madrid tavern serves great value wines and generous portions of splendid *tapas*. Booking is recommended. ✆ *Calle General Lacy 14 • Map F6 • 91 467 8458 • Closed Easter; Mon L Jun–Oct; Sun D & Mon Nov–May • €*

Note: *Unless otherwise stated, all restaurants accept credit cards and serve vegetarian meals.*

Left **Café Gijón** Right **Calle de Serrano**

Salamanca and Recoletos

ONE OF MADRID'S MOST AFFLUENT NEIGHBOURHOODS, *Salamanca is named after its founder, José de Salamanca y Mayol (1811–83). The Marquis first saw the commercial possibilities of the area bordering the Retiro in the 1860s and transformed it into a model of urban planning, with grid-patterned streets and elegant mansions. The new neighbourhood was an immediate hit with the upper classes who found the central districts stifling and their own antiquated homes lacking in such mod-cons as flushing toilets and hot running water. Salamanca soon acquired a reputation as a bastion of conservatism and its residents were among the most loyal supporters of the Franco regime. Today the streets around Calle de Serrano, Calle de Goya and Calle de Velázquez form Madrid's premier shopping district and showcase some of Spain's leading fashion designers. The prices, though, may leave you breathless – shopaholics take note.*

Plaza de Colón

🔟 Sights

Sign up for DK's email newsletter on traveldk.com

1 Café Gijón

The haunt of journalists and leading cultural figures, the Gijón was founded in 1888 and is one of the few surviving *tertulia* cafés where, traditionally, men gathered to discuss issues of the day. Former patrons include the poet Federico García Lorca, the American film director Orson Welles and – more improbably – the famous Dutch spy and belly-dancer, Mata Hari. Order *tapas* and drinks at the bar or book a table for lunch. The windows look on to Paseo de Recoletos where the café has its own terrace.
Ⓢ *Paseo de Recoletos 21 • Map F3 • €€*

2 Museo Arqueológico Nacional

The scale of the Archaeological Museum's collections can be daunting, so home in on what interests you most. The star turn on the main floor is the *Lady of Elche*, a stone bust of an Iberian noblewoman from the 4th century BC. There is a niche in the back to hold the ashes of the dead, which is typical of the funerary rites of Iberian culture. Other highlights include a Roman mosaic floor representing two gladiators, the Recesvinth crown from the Guarrazar treasure (Toledo, 7th-century), and an ivory cross from the church of San Isidoro in León (1063). There is also a collection of amphorae from ancient Greece. Some parts of the museum are closed for renovations. During this time the museum is hosting a free exhibition from Madrid-born photographer José Manuel Ballester (b.1960) whose works focus on architectonic spaces.
Ⓢ *Calle Serrano 13 • Map G3 • Open 9:30am–8pm Tue–Sat, 9:30am–3pm Sun & public hols • Closed 1 Jan, 6 Jan, 1 May, 15 May, 24 Dec, 25 Dec, 31 Dec • Free during the renovations*

Plaza de Colón

3 Plaza de Colón

Named after Christopher Columbus, this expansive square, commemorates the discovery of the New World. The three monumental slabs near Calle de Serrano were designed by Joaquín Vaquero Turcíos to symbolize the ships that made the voyage to America in 1492. There is also a more conventional sculpture of Columbus, erected in the 19th century. The base shows Queen Isabel of Castile selling her jewellery to finance the trip. Ⓢ *Map F2*

4 Museo Lázaro Galdiano

José Lázaro Galdiano (1862–1947) was a distinguished patron of the arts and collector whose Italian-style palazzo is now a museum showcasing his fabulous possessions. There are Spanish works by El Greco, Zurbarán, Murillo, Velázquez and Goya and European paintings by Reynolds, Constable and Gains-borough. There are also spectacular *objets d'art (see p45)*.
Ⓢ *Calle Serrano 122 • Metro Rubén Darío or Gregorio Marañón • Open 10am–4:30pm Wed–Sat, 10am–3pm Sun • Closed public hols • Adm (free 3:30–4:30pm Mon & Wed–Sat, 2–3pm Sun)*

Museo de Escultura al Aire Libre

Situated beneath a road bridge, the open-air sculpture museum is easily overlooked. Nevertheless, exhibited in its windswept precincts are works by a number of outstanding modern Spanish sculptors, including Eduardo Chillída, Julio González, Joan Miró and Pablo Serrano. 🖎 *Paseo de la Castellana • Map G1*

Fundación Juan March

One of Spain's most vital cultural institutions was founded in 1955 by the banker Juan March Ordinas, to promote contemporary Spanish art. Madrid shares the permanent collection, especially strong on abstract artists of the 1950s

Museo de Escultura al Aire Libre

such as Tàpies, Sempere, Saura, and Millares, with other branches of the foundation in Cuenca and Palma de Mallorca, but the foundation's main attraction is its outstanding temporary exhibitions *(see p57)*. 🖎 *Castelló 77 • Map H1 • Open 11am–8pm Mon–Sat, 10am–2pm Sun & public hols • Free*

Paseo de Recoletos

"Paseo" implies a stroll and this lovely avenue, at its best on a sunny morning or just after sunset, was designed precisely for that purpose. The first cafés began to appear in the 19th century when the boulevard was nicknamed "Recoletos beach". Most of the originals had disappeared by the 1980s when the Movida gave the terraces a new lease of life *(see pp42–3)*. The Pabellón de Espejo looks the part with its painted tiles and wrought-iron adornments but actually dates from the 1990s. No. 10 was the residence of the Marqués de Salamanca. 🖎 *Map F3*

Calle de Serrano

Madrid's smartest shopping street runs through the heart of the Salamanca district. Here, top Spanish designer names such as Loewe, Purificación García and Roberto Verino rub shoulders with Armani, Gucci, Yves Saint Laurent and Cartier. Even if you're not especially interested in fashion, there's plenty to amuse you. Madrid's best-known department store, El Corte Inglés, has branches at Nos. 47 and 52, while Agatha Ruíz de la Prada is at No. 27. If you're looking for gifts, visit Adolfo Domínguez's concept store (No. 5), which stocks great gifts, jewellery and accessories. For a bite to eat, try Serrano 50 which has a *menú del día* as well as *tapas*. 🖎 *Map G3*

Fundación Juan March

Calle de Hermosilla
This side-street off Serrano has everything from cut-glass decanters to beach bags. For designer clothes for children, try Nanos (No. 21). For a cocktail, visit the Dry Cosmopolitan Bar opened by the mixicologist Javier de las Muelas at the Gran Melia Fenix Hotel (No. 2), or pick up quirky souvenirs from Tiger (No. 91). Estay *(see p84)* is just the spot for lunch. Next door but one is Tea Shop (No. 48), with more than 40 aromatic teas, including rum, toffee, cherry and passion fruit. ◈ *Map G2*

Museo Sorolla
This museum is devoted to the Valencian artist Joaquín Sorolla y Bastida (1863–1923) who spent the last 13 years of his life here. Some rooms have been left as they were in his lifetime, while others are used to hang his work. Dubbed "the Spanish Impressionist", his subject matter ranges from Spanish folk types to landscapes, but Sorolla is at his most appealing when evoking the sea. Don't leave without seeing the Andalusian-style garden.
◈ *Paseo del General Martínez Campos 37 • Metro Iglesia, Rubén Darío or Gregorio Marañón • Open 9:30am–8pm Tue–Sat, 10am–3pm Sun & public hols • Closed some public hols • Adm*

A Day's Shopping

Morning

Leave Serrano metro station, heading south and limber up with a spot of window shopping on Salamanca's main fashion drag. Turn left into Calle Columela – try not to pay too much attention to **Mallorca's** mouthwatering displays of cakes and pastries *(see p82)* – then left again into Calle Claudio Coello, a delightful street lined with private art galleries, antique shops and boutiques. Don't miss Capa Sculptures (No. 19), Monasterio Antigüedades (No. 21), **Cristina Castañer** (No. 51) and stylish concept store **Isolee** (No. 55) *(see p83)*. Look left at Calle de Goya for the entrance to the shopping mall, **El Jardín de Serrano** *(see p82)*. Cross Goya, then continue along Calle de Claudio Coello to **Calle de Hermosilla**.

As many Spanish shops take a long lunch break, this is the perfect moment to stop for lunch. Choices abound, but leading contenders include **Teatríz** for more formal eating, the *tapas* bar at **Estay** *(see p84)* or **Gino's** *(see p85)* for good value Italian food.

Afternoon

When you're ready to move on, take a walk along the vibrant thoroughfare of Calle Jorge Juan, which boasts designer names such as **Pedro Garcia**, **Kenzo** and **Loewe**. At Calle de Ayala turn left to return to **Calle de Serrano**, Madrid's boutique boulevard, where you can either ogle over the designer goods and dream, or blow your budget on a beautiful handbag or pair of shoes.

Left **Calle de Serrano shops** Right **Santa**

Top 10 General Shops

1 El Corte Inglés
This branch of Madrid's best known department store also has a beauty parlour, restaurant and supermarket as well as the usual individual departments.
§ *Calle de Goya 76–87 • Map H2*

2 El Jardín de Serrano
One of Madrid's most exclusive shopping malls. It has the top names in fashion, accessories and jewellery as well as a branch of the Mallorca cafeteria and delicatessen chain.
§ *Calle de Goya 6–8 • Map G2*

3 Galería ABC Serrano
Salamanca's other main shopping centre also has a good selection of boutiques (including a branch of the Spanish chain, Mango). § *Calle de Serrano 61 • Map G1*

4 Centro de Anticuarios Lagasca
Antiques-lovers can save time traipsing the streets for individual shops by visiting this gallery which brings together a number of Madrid's most reputable dealers. § *Calle de Lagasca 36 • Map G3*

5 Santa
If you're a chocolate lover, look no further than this tiny outlet on Serrano which also sells gift-wrapped sweets. The speciality here is *leña vieja* (chocolates that are cast to resemble tree trunks). § *Calle de Serrano 56 • Map G1*

6 Mercado de la Paz
Salamanca's best known food market is hidden away on this side street and is worth tracking down for its Spanish delicacies and a good range of international cheese selections.
§ *Calle de Ayala 28 • Map G2*

7 Vázquez Fruits
Only small but this famous fruit vendor includes, it is said, Queen Sofía among its patrons. The selection of tropical fruits in particular will stir the taste buds.
§ *Calle de Ayala 11 • Map G2*

8 Mallorca
This reputable delicatessen chain offers a mouthwatering selection of cheeses, hams, pastries, filled rolls, cakes and ice creams. There's a small bar if you can't tear yourself away.
§ *Calle de Serrano 6 • Map G3*

9 Álvarez Gómez
This firm has been in the perfume business for more than a century, selling its own line of eau de cologne. Also top brand names like Chanel and Estée Lauder and Bulgari jewellery.
§ *Calle de Serrano 14 • Map G3*

10 Zara Home
Part of the Inditex Group, which also includes the clothing brand of the same name, Zara Home stocks a great range of stylish and affordable household goods. You can shop online too.
§ *Calle Serrano 88 • Map G1*

Left **Adolfo Domínguez** Right **Agatha Ruíz de la Prada**

🔟 Fashion Shops

Adolfo Domínguez
This flagship store showcases the collections of one of Spain's leading designers, famous for elegant understatement. It also hosts concerts and exhibitions.
🕲 *Calle de Serrano 5 • Map G1–3*

Agatha Ruíz de la Prada
Men and women's fashions by one of the country's most original designers, noted for her daring use of colour. Her name can also be found on the accessories, stationery and household goods sold here.
🕲 *Calle de Serrano 27 • Map G2*

Purificación García
The minimalist layout of the store is the perfect backdrop for the Spanish designer's sleek men's and women's clothing. Good range of accessories.
🕲 *Calle de Serrano 28 • Map G1–3*

Loewe
Loewe may not sound Spanish, but is in fact one of Spain's longest established names – the first Madrid store opened in 1846. Renowned for accessories, especially leather.
🕲 *Calle de Serrano 26 & 34 • Map G3*

Roberto Verino
Men's and women's fashions and accessories by another of Spain's flagship designers. Claims to cater for confident women who know what they want to wear.
🕲 *Calle de Serrano 33 • Map G3*

Angel Schlesser
Like Roberto Verino, Spanish designer Angel Schlesser was labelled "dissident" but has now moved into the mainstream with his distinctive style of clothes and accessories for men and women. Trademarks include low-key colours and attention to detail. 🕲 *Calle de Don Ramón de la Cruz 2 • Map G2*

Speed and Bacon
This great studio sells shoes, clothes and accessories from up-and-coming Spanish artists and designers such as La Condesa, Yiyi Gutz, Yono Taolo and Leticia Vea. 🕲 *Calle Don Ramón de la Cruz 26 • Map G2*

Ursula Mascaro
Head to this flagship store where you can discover the flamboyant shoe and handbag designs of Ursula Mascaro.
🕲 *Claudio Coello 83 • Map G3*

Cristina Castañer
Espadrilles are not usually associated with high fashion, but this Spanish designer has turned them into an art form. All colours and styles from casual to evening wear. 🕲 *Calle de Claudio Coello 51 • Map G3*

Isolee
One of Madrid's first concept stores, Isolee mixes fashion, design and gourmet food all under one roof. 🕲 *Calle de Claudio Coello 55 • Map G3*

Left **José Luis** Right **Tasca La Farmacia**

Tabernas, Bars and Cafés

1 Tasca La Farmacia
This former pharmacy has attractive *azulejo* tile decoration. The house speciality is *bacalao* (cod) prepared in many different ways *(see p66)*. ⚲ Calle de Diego de León 9 • Map G1 • 91 564 8652 • Closed Sun, late Jul–late Aug • €€

2 Vino Tinto
Part of a chain, this modern grill-style *taberna* offers simple dishes such as steaks and burgers and a good selection of wines. ⚲ Jorge Juan 8 • Map G3 • 91 140 3417 • Closed Sun D • €€€

3 José Luis
Attracting a loyal clientele, the *tapas* here are said to be among the best in the city. The tortilla is heavenly. ⚲ Calle de Serrano 89 • Map G2 • 91 563 0958 • €€€

4 Taberna La Daniela
This traditional *azulejo*-decorated *taberna* serves a tempting *tapas* selection. The three-course *cocido* (Madrid stew) is also worth trying. ⚲ Calle de General Pardiñas 21 • Metro Goya • 91 575 23 29 • €€

5 El Rincón de Goya
Decorated with scenes of old Madrid, this popular local serves standards such as the Madrid stew *cocido*. ⚲ Calle de Lagasca 46 • Map G2 • 91 576 38 89 • €

6 El Espejo
You can choose between the main restaurant or the elegant terrace and conservatory. The terrace only serves a set menu or *tapas*, and a pianist will serenade you during the summer. ⚲ Paseo de Recoletos 31 • Map F3 • 91 319 1122 • Closed 24 Dec • €€€€

7 Estay
A bar with a touch of sophistication, Estay offers a selection of imaginatively prepared *tapas* such as French toast with apple compote. The desserts are to die for. ⚲ Calle de Hermosilla 46 • Map G2 • 91 578 0470 • Closed Sun • €€

8 O'Caldiño
This classic tapas bar serves delicious seafood in an elegant setting. ⚲ Calle Lagasca 74 • Map G2 • 91 575 7014 • Closed 1 Jan, 25 Dec • €€

9 Mallorca
This branch of the popular Mallorca chain serves canapés, quiche and other delicious savoury pastries. ⚲ Calle de Serrano 6, Velázquez 59 • Map G3 • 91 577 1859 • €€

10 Ramsés
The super-stylish main restaurant at Ramsés serves an eclectic mix of international dishes. ⚲ Plaza de la Independencia 4 • Map G3 • 91 435 1666 • €€€€

JOCKEY

Price Categories

For a three-course meal for one with half a bottle of wine (or equivalent meal), taxes and extra charges.

€ under €25
€€ €25–€35
€€€ €35–€55
€€€€ €55–€70
€€€€€ over €70

Above **Jockey**

🔟 Restaurants

1 Pan de Lujo
Housed within an old bread factory, this restaurant has a trendy urban feel. Try the burgers or grilled octopus. ✎ *Calle Jorge Juan 20 • Map G3 • 91 436 1100 • €€€€*

2 Jockey
Winner of numerous culinary awards including a Michelin star, Jockey is one of Madrid's best and most expensive restaurants. Seasonal game and wild fowl dishes are a highlight when they are in season. ✎ *Calle de Amador de los Ríos 6 • Map F2 • 91 310 0411 • Closed Sun, Aug, public hols • €€€€*

3 La Trainera
Renowned for its fish and seafood. The well thought out Spanish wine selection beautifully complements the fresh daily catches from Galicia. ✎ *Calle de Lagasca 60 • Map G3 • 91 576 8035 • Closed Sun, 1 Jan, Aug, 25 Dec • €€€€*

4 La Galette
Vegetarian cooking is slowly catching on in Madrid, thanks to places like this. It has a cosy candle-lit ambience and country-kitchen decor. ✎ *Conde de Aranda 11 • Map G3 • 91 576 0641 • Closed Sun D, Aug • €€*

5 Gino's
A popular Italian restaurant chain, Gino's offers a wide selection of pizzas, pasta and meat dishes. Especially good value are the midweek all-inclusive meals for two. ✎ *Calle de Hermosilla 23 • Map G2 • 91 275 8961 • €*

6 Al-Mounia
North African specialities are served at this well-established restaurant. ✎ *Calle de Recoletos 5 • Map G3 • 91 435 0828 • Closed Sun, Easter, Aug • €€€€*

7 El Borbollón
Dine on traditional French Basque dishes such as rack of lamb. ✎ *Calle Recoletos 7 • Map F3 • 91 431 4134 • Closed Sat L, Sun, public hols • €€€*

8 Teatriz
The restaurant was designed by Philippe Starck. The menu is Mediterranean. ✎ *Calle de Hermosilla 15 • Map G2 • 91 577 5379 • €€€€*

9 Ramón Freixa Madrid
Star chef Ramón Freixa's gastronomic mecca received its second Michelin star in 2010. ✎ *Calle Claudio Coello 67 • Map G3 • 91 781 8262 • Closed Sun, Mon, Easter, Aug, Christmas • €€€€€*

10 Iroco
This is Spanish cuisine with a range of influences. Diners pay extra to sit on the terrace. ✎ *Calle de Velázquez 18 • Map G3 • 91 431 7381 • €€€*

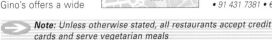

Note: Unless otherwise stated, all restaurants accept credit cards and serve vegetarian meals

Around Town – Salamanca & Recoletos

85

Left **Círculo de Bellas Artes** Right **Tío Pepe sign, Puerta del Sol**

Downtown Madrid

CENTRAL MADRID BEGAN TO TAKE ON ITS PRESENT APPEARANCE *in the mid-19th century with the modernization of Puerta del Sol. This busy intersection was the first to have electric street lighting, trams and, in 1919, Madrid's first underground station. Meanwhile Calle de Alcalá was becoming the focal point of a new financial district as banks, insurance offices and other businesses set up their headquarters in showy new premises. Building work on the Gran Vía began in 1910 but was only completed in the 1940s with the remodelling of Plaza de España. To make way for this sweeping Parisian-style boulevard, 1,315 m (1,440 yds) long and designed with automobile traffic in mind, more than 300 buildings were demolished and 14 streets disappeared altogether. The new avenue reflected the American architectural tastes of the jazz age, with skyscrapers, cinemas, glitzy cocktail bars, luxury hotels, theatres and restaurants.*

Telefónica

Sights

1. Puerta del Sol
2. Real Casa de la Aduana
3. Real Academia de Bellas Artes
4. Círculo de Bellas Artes
5. Edificio Telefónica
6. El Corte Inglés
7. Metrópolis
8. Banco de España
9. Plaza del Callao
10. Casino de Madrid

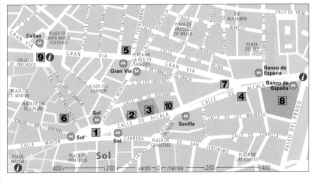

Share your travel recommendations on traveldk.com

1 Puerta del Sol

Ten streets radiate from this elliptical square, which for most *madrileños* is the real heart of the city. The name means "Gateway of the Sun" although the actual gateway was demolished in 1570. Of numerous historic events to take place here, the most dramatic occurred during the 1808 insurrection when snipers fired on one of Napoleon's soldiers, provoking a massacre. Dominating the south side of the square is the 18th-century Casa de Correos, a post office which later became the Ministry of the Interior and now houses the regional government. A marker in front of the building indicates *"kilómetro cero"*, from which all distances in Spain are calculated. In the centre of the square is a statue of Carlos III and, on the corner of Calle del Carmen, a bronze statue of a bear climbing an arbutus tree, the symbol of the city. ✪ *Map N4*

2 Real Casa de la Aduana

The royal customs house was a cornerstone of Carlos III's plans to improve the appearance of the city. In 1761 the queen's stables and 16 houses were demolished to make way for Francesco Sabatini's Neo-Classical masterpiece. Huge amounts of money were lavished on the façade alone, the decorative features of which include ashlar columns and a balcony

Façade detail, Real Casa de la Aduana

Street sign, Puerta del Sol

bearing the royal coat of arms. It is now home to the Ministry of Finance. ✪ *Calle de Alcalá 5, 7, 9 & 11 • Map P4 • Closed to public*

3 Real Academia de Bellas Artes

Founded in the 18th century, the palatial Academy of Fine Arts houses a collection of paintings surpassed only by the Prado and the Thyssen-Bornemisza. Outstanding among the Spanish paintings are the Goyas, including the classic fiesta scene *Burial of the Sardine*. There are also impressive works by European masters including Bellini, Tintoretto, Van Dyck, Rubens and Titian. Picasso and Dalí studied here for a time. ✪ *Calle de Alcalá 13 • Map P3 • Open 9am–3pm Tue–Sat, 9am–2:30pm Sun & public hols • Closed Mon • Adm*

4 Círculo de Bellas Artes

While the golden age of the Arts Club was in the 1920s and 1930s, this cultural organization is still thriving today. The Círculo promotes Spanish and world culture, with exhibitions, theatre and ballet productions, art films, workshops and conferences. It even has a magazine and a radio station. ✪ *Calle Alcalá 42 • Map R3 • Open 10am–9pm daily (café open until 1am); Exhibitions: 11am–7pm Tue–Sat, 11am–2pm Sun • Exhibitions closed in Aug • Adm*

Edificio Telefónica
5 Now headquarters of Spain's national telephone company, this was Madrid's first high-rise building. Designed by American architect Lewis Weeks in 1929, it reflects the values of the Chicago School then much in vogue. The Telefónica building played an important role in the Civil War when it was used by the Republican army as a vantage point for observing enemy troop movements in the Casa de Campo. Conversely, Franco's forces found it an ideal range finder for their artillery. The Fundación de Arte y Tecnología Telefónica has an exhibition on the history of communications as well as a splendid art collection, with works by Picasso, Juan Gris, Eduardo Chillida and Antoni Tàpies. Another room on the ground floor hosts temporary exhibitions. ◎ *Calle Gran Vía 28 • Map P2 • Open 10am–2pm, 5–8pm Tue–Fri, 11am–8pm Sat, 10am–2pm Sun & public hols • Free*

El Corte Inglés
6 The story of the founder of Spain's premier department store, Ramón Areces Rodríguez, is a classic tale of rags-to-riches. Areces emigrated to Cuba aged 15 and worked as a shop assistant before returning to Spain in 1934. The following year he

El Corte Inglés

opened a small tailor's in Calle de Preciados and never looked back. It's hard to miss the distinctive white shopping bags with the green logo. The store at Preciados No.1 sells CDs, No. 2 stocks over half a million books, No.3 specializes in fashion and No. 9 has sports gear. There are numerous branches in the capital. ◎ *Calle de Preciados • Map N3*

Metrópolis
7 It was La Unión y el Fénix insurance company, the original owners of this Madrid landmark, who commissioned the striking statue on the cupola. Known as *"Ave Fenix"*, it represents the fabled Egyptian bird which died on a funeral pyre but rose from the flames once every 500 years. When the Metrópolis company moved into the building, they

Metrópolis

inherited the sculpture which then lost its significance *(see p46)*. ✆ *Corner Gran Vía & Calle de Alcalá • Map R3*

8 Banco de España
The Bank of Spain was founded in 1856 and 20 years later acquired the exclusive right to issue bank notes in its name. The most impressive part of these headquarters is the corner section, decorated with typical Neo-Baroque ornamentation – caryatids and medallions, a marble clock and the distinctive golden globe. Spain's gold reserves are locked away in the vaults beneath Plaza de Cibeles. Apart from gold, the bank's main treasure is its art collection, with works ranging from Goya to Tàpies. It can only be viewed by written application to the bank.
✆ *Calle de Alcalá 48 • Map F4*

9 Plaza del Callao
The look of this busy square reflects the sleek modernist architecture of 1930s America. Good examples are the Edificio Cine Callao (No. 3), the Palacio de la Prensa (No. 4), the former headquarters of the Press Association, and the Palacio de la Música (Gran Vía 35), which today houses both the Cine Capitol cinema *(see p92)* and the Hotel Vincci Capitol. ✆ *Map M2*

10 Casino de Madrid
This exclusive gentlemen's club was founded in 1910. The florid architecture by Luis Esteve and José López Salaberry is typical of the period, but unfortunately the lavish interior is rarely open to the public. Non-members, however, are allowed in the restaurant, La Terraza Del Casino, which has one Michelin star.
✆ *Calle de Alcalá 15 • Map Q3*

A Day's Stroll Around Downtown Madrid

Morning

🕐 Start the walk outside the Casa de Correos in **Puerta del Sol** *(see p87)*, a popular meeting point for *madrileños*. Cross the square in the direction of the bus stops, then turn on to Calle de Alcalá. This busy street is lined with fine examples of 18th- and 19th-century architecture. Two examples on your left are the **Casa de la Aduana** and the **Real Academia de Bellas Artes** *(see p87)*. Take time to visit this often overlooked gallery, with its small, but quality, collection of paintings. Next door is the showy façade of the **Casino de Madrid**.

☕ Cross Calle de Alcalá when you reach the junction with Gran Vía, then head for coffee in the **Círculo de Bellas Artes** *(see p87)*. As you make your way back to Gran Vía look up to admire the **Metrópolis** building, then take a stroll along Madrid's bustling main avenue.

🍴 When you're ready for lunch, escape the crowds by turning into Calle de Hortaleza, then Calle de la Reina. At No. 29 is **La Barraca**, famous for its *paellas*.

Afternoon

Head back to Gran Vía and continue to **Plaza del Callao**. Turn left into Calle de Preciados, a pedestrianized street dominated by two large department stores, FNAC and **El Corte Inglés**. After a leisurely browse around the shops, return to Puerta del Sol as it begins to liven up for the evening.

➔ *Following pages* **Plaza de Cibeles at night (see p73)**

Left **Caixa Forum** Right **Teatro Lírico Nacional de la Zarzuela**

10 Cinemas and Entertainment

1 Cine Estudio Círculo de Bellas Artes
The cinema of the fine arts centre *(see p87)* shows classic movies by 20th-century directors such as Eisenstein, Fassbinder, Francis Ford Coppola and John Huston. ✆ *Calle de Alcalá 42 • Map E4*

2 Yelmo Cines Ideal
This multiplex cinema with nine screens (including 3D) shows original language movies with subtitles. Discounts on Mondays. ✆ *Calle Doctor Cortezo • Map N5*

3 Cines Renoir
European independent cinema is projected onto the five screens. Each film is shown in its original language with Spanish subtitles. A great location on Calle Princesa. ✆ *Calle Princesa 3 • Map B3*

4 Cine Capitol
Located in the Art Deco Carrión building, this cinema's greatest moment occurred early in the Civil War when Eisenstein's stirring movie *Kronstadt* was shown to an audience including the President of the Republic and leading military figures. Films are screened in Spanish. There are three screens that include digital 3D technology. ✆ *Gran Vía 41 • Map M2*

5 Caixa Forum
This art centre is based in one of the area's few industrial buildings. The site has a cinema and space for exhibitions, concerts, festivals and conferences. ✆ *Paseo del Prado 36 • Map F5*

6 Teatro Lírico Nacional de la Zarzuela
Purpose-built to showcase Spain's unique light opera form, *Zarzuela*. Also international opera, music recitals and other events *(see p56)*. ✆ *Calle de Jovellanos 4 • Map R4*

7 Teatro Lope de Vega
Musicals like *Beauty and the Beast* and *The Lion King* are staged here, performed in Spanish. ✆ *Gran Vía 57 • Map Q3*

8 Teatro María Guerrero
This theatre is home to the National Dramatic Centre. The company stages hugely successful theatre plays and is a favourite amongst theatre-goers. ✆ *Calle de Tamayo y Baus 4 • Map F3 • Dis. access*

9 Gula Gula
Great views of the Gran Vía and Alcalá can be had from the first floor of this restaurant, which entertains customers with disco music and floor shows in the evenings. ✆ *Gran Vía 1 • Map R3*

10 El Sol
Venue for concerts by Spanish and international bands that date from the Movida period *(see pp42–3)*. Reasonable bar and entry prices. ✆ *Calle de los Jardines 3 • Map P3 • Closed Sun & Mon*

Left **Zara** Right **Cortefiel**

🔟 Downtown Shops

1 Zara
This Spanish fashion pheno-
menon is now also a household
name throughout Europe and the
United States. Stylish clothes for
all the family at very reasonable
prices. ✆ *Gran Vía 34 • Map N2*

2 FNAC
This useful store, just a few
minutes' walk from Puerta del
Sol, sells everything from CDs
and sound systems to cameras,
videos, books and mobile
phones. Helpful floor staff, some
of whom speak a little English.
✆ *Calle de Preciados 28 • Map N3*

3 Horno San Onofre
The decoration of this
traditional Madrid bakery borders
on the palatial. The produce is
just as good – every conceivable
type of bread, as well as
seasonal specialities such as
roscón de Reyes and *turrón (see
p55)*. ✆ *Calle de S Onofre 3 • Map P2*

4 Cortefiel
This branch of the Spanish
high street chain specializes in
reasonably priced clothes and
sportswear for both men and
women. ✆ *Gran Vía 27 • Map Q3*

5 O2
Raid this store near Puerta
del Sol for glitzy costume
jewellery and equally showy
accessories – perfect for a night
on the town. Head for the first
floor for imaginative gift ideas.
✆ *Calle del Carmen 8 • Map N3*

6 Casa del Libro
Four floors of books on
every subject under the sun.
Some English books. Good travel
section, especially for books on
Spain. ✆ *Gran Vía 29 • Map Q3*

7 Loewe
If you are a fan of the
Spanish brand Loewe, then head
to Gran Vía 8. This is the original
store that opened in 1939.
Check out its guestbook whose
lustrous signatories include
Grace Kelly. ✆ *Gran Vía 8 • Map E4*

8 El Elefante Blanco
Shades of the Big Top in this
small shop, founded by a former
circus performer. Sells all the
paraphernalia – stilts, jugglers
clubs, diabolos, etc. Great for
kids. ✆ *Calle de las Infantas 5 • Map R2*

9 VIPS
This useful shopping and
restaurant chain is open almost
all hours. You can eat in the
reasonably priced café-
restaurant, while the shop stocks
everything from books and
newspapers to drinks and
batteries. ✆ *Gran Vía 43 • Map Q3*

10 Grassy
This famous jeweller
occupies one of the signature
buildings of the Gran Vía dating
from 1916. The gleaming window
displays of rings, watches and
other items (all original designs)
are equally distinguished. ✆ *Gran
Vía 1 • Map R3*

Left **Artemisa** Right **Casa Labra**

Places to Eat and Drink

1 Casa Labra
A Madrid institution, it was here that Pablo Iglesias founded the Spanish Socialist party in 1879. Of the *tapas* on offer try the house speciality, *soldaditos de Pavía* (fried cod). 🅢 *Calle de Tetuán 12 • Map N4 • 91 531 0081 • €€*

2 Artemisa
This well-known vegetarian restaurant features a nettle purée among other imaginative dishes. It has organic wines and herbal teas. 🅢 *Calle de las Tres Cruces 4 • Map P3 • 91 521 8721 • €€*

3 El Escarpín
This lively Asturian tavern serves regional specialities such as bean soup *(fabada)* and sausages in cider *(chorizo a la sidra)*. 🅢 *Calle de las Hileras 17 • Map M3 • 91 559 9957 • €€*

4 Fatigas del Querer
This Andalusian tavern was built in 1920. There is an excellent range of *tapas* on offer, including hearty *raciones*, Iberian ham, seafood and fresh, fried fish. The atmosphere is always lively, especially at night *(see p47)*. 🅢 *Calle de la Cruz 17 • Map P4 • 91 523 2131 • No credit cards • €*

5 Estado Puro
This busy, stylish restaurant run by famous chef Paco Roncero, offers a creative renewal of classic Spanish tapas. 🅢 *Plaza Cánovas del Castillo 4 • Map F5 • 91 330 2400 • Closed Sun D • €€*

6 Museo Chicote
Ernest Hemingway put this cocktail bar on the map in the 1930s; other famous visitors were Frank Sinatra and Orson Welles *(see p64)*. 🅢 *Gran Vía 12 • Map Q3 • 91 532 6737 • Closed Sun, Aug • €€*

7 La Gloria de Montera
The fusion Mediterranean cuisine is good value for money. Arrive early. 🅢 *Calle Caballero de Gracia 10 • Map Q3 • 91 523 4407 • Closed 1 Jan, 24 Dec, 25 Dec, 31 Dec • No reservations • €€*

8 Cock
This tastefully decorated late-night bar is a good place to round off the evening. 🅢 *Calle de la Reina 16 • Map R3 • 91 532 2826 • €€*

9 Museo del Jamón
Snack on delicious cold cuts, cheeses, cakes and sandwiches at this restaurant and delicatessen. 🅢 *Carrera de San Jerónimo 6 • Map P4 • 91 521 0346 • €*

10 Café & Té
The name "coffee and tea" says it all. Branch of a cafeteria chain in the heart of theatre land *(see p92)*. 🅢 *Gran Vía 42 • Map N2 • 91 523 2330 • No credit cards • €*

Recommend your favourite restaurant on traveldk.com

Above **Zara**

Price Categories

For a three-course meal for one with half a bottle of wine (or equivalent meal), taxes and extra charges.

€	under €25
€€	€25–€35
€€€	€35–€55
€€€€	€55–€70
€€€€€	over €70

📙 Specialist Restaurants

1 Zara
Just off the Gran Vía, Zara has been a rallying point for Cuban exiles since the 1960s. It serves Caribbean standards like *ropa vieja* (stewed meat in tomato sauce) and great daiquiris. ✎ *Calle de las Infantas 5 • Map R2 • 91 532 2074 • Closed Sat, Sun, public hols, Aug, • €€*

2 Al Natural
At this unpretentious eatery that serves vegetarian dishes the house speciality is spinach and mushroom tart *(tarta de setas y espinacas)*. ✎ *Calle de Zorilla 11 • Map R4 • 91 369 4709 • Closed Sun D • €*

3 Cornucopia
This American-run, art-filled restaurant gives transatlantic treatment to Spanish fare, with special cheap menus and great desserts. ✎ *Calle Navas de Tolosa 9 • Map M4 • 91 521 3896 • €*

4 Edelweiss
Next to the Chamber of Deputies, this restaurant is popular with visiting German politicians for its central European cooking. The speciality is knuckle of pork with puréed potatoes. ✎ *Calle de Jovellanos 7 • Map R4 • 91 532 3383 • Closed Sun D • €€€*

5 Errota-Zar
This family-run restaurant serves grilled meat and fish dishes cooked to perfection. Try the red bream *(besugo)*. ✎ *Calle de Jovellanos 3, 1st floor • Map R4 • 91 531 2564 • Closed Sun, Easter • €€€€*

6 Ferpal
This charcuterie near Sol has the usual range of *jamón Ibérico*, pâtés and cheeses, as well as sandwiches. Eat at the bar or take away. ✎ *Calle de Arenal 7 • Map R4 • 91 532 3899 • Closed Sun • €*

7 Daniel Sorlut Oyster Bar
Enjoy the atmosphere of this buzzing gourmet market and sample some of the best oysters in town. ✎ *Mercado San Miguel • Map C4 • 91 559 1041 • €€*

8 Don Pelayo
Asturian cooking is on offer in this formal restaurant. There is live music on Fridays and Saturdays. ✎ *Calle de Alcalá 33 • Map R3 • 91 531 0031 • Closed Sun • €€€*

9 La Pecera
For a small entrance fee you can enjoy tea in the café of the Círculo de Bellas Artes. ✎ *Calle Alcalá 42 • Map R3 • 91 360 5400 • €*

10 Lhardy
At this Madrid institution some customers never get further than the *tapas* counter downstairs *(see p68)*. ✎ *Carrera de San Jerónimo 8 • Map P4 • 91 522 2207 • Closed Sun & public hols D • €€€€*

Left **Palacio Real** Right **Teatro Real**

Royal Madrid

TO WANDER AROUND THIS PART OF MADRID *is to be constantly reminded of its regal associations. The Monasterio de las Descalzas Reales and the Monasterio de la Encarnación are both royal foundations, dating from the Habsburg era, while work on the Palacio Real began in the reign of Felipe V. Joseph Bonaparte was king of Spain for only four years (1808–12), but he laid the plans for the Plaza de Oriente. Further afield, the Ermita de San Antonio de la Florida was commissioned by Carlos IV.*

🔟 Sights

1. Palacio Real
2. Monasterio de las Descalzas Reales
3. Museo de América
4. Museo Cerralbo
5. Ermita de San Antonio de la Florida
6. Monasterio de la Encarnación
7. Teatro Real
8. Catedral de la Almudena
9. Plaza de Oriente
10. Plaza de España

Catedral de la Almudena

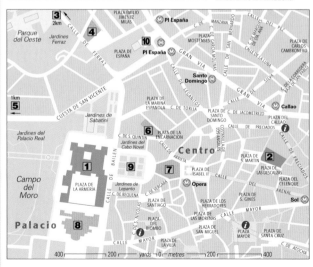

1 Palacio Real

Spain's magnificent Royal Palace dominates the landscape in this part of the city, its sparkling, colonnaded façade looking out on to the lush grounds of the Campo del Moro *(see pp8–11)*.

2 Monasterio de las Descalzas Reales

This 16th-century former royal palace and convent is a treasure trove of art and sculpture *(see pp20–21)*.

3 Museo de América

Spain's links with the American continent have a long history, and this wonderful museum displays artifacts from all eras *(see pp34–5)*.

4 Museo Cerralbo

Don Enrique de Aguilera y Gamboa, Marqués de Cerralbo (1845–1922) was a poet, a politician and a compulsive collector, searching the world for artistic treasures that would adorn his palatial home. He bequeathed his collection to the state so that it could be enjoyed by others. Highlights include a majolica Nativity by Renaissance artist Andrea della Robbia (Porcelain Room) and El Greco's *Ecstasy of St Francis* (Sacristy), but the *pièce de*

Queen's Bedroom, Palacio Real

résistance is Juderías Caballero's *History of Dance* in the dome of the ballroom *(see p44)*. ✎ Calle de Ventura Rodríguez 17 • Map J1 • Open 9:30am–3pm Tue–Sat, 5–8pm Thu, 10am–3pm Sun & public hols • Dis. access • Adm (free 2–3pm Sat, 5–8pm Thu)

5 Ermita de San Antonio de la Florida

The hermitage dedicated to St Anthony of Padua was completed in 1798. Goya began work on his sublime frescoes in June, and by December they were finished. On St Anthony's Day (13 June) unmarried girls would come to the hermitage to ask the saint to find them a husband. ✎ Glorieta de San Antonio de la Florida 5 • Open 9:30am–8pm Tue–Fri, 10am–2pm Sat & Sun • Closed Mon, public hols • Dis. access • Free

Monasterio de las Descalzas Reales

You may find binoculars useful for viewing the Goya frescoes in the Ermita de San Antonio de la Florida.

The Virgin of Almudena

A niche in the wall next to the cathedral contains a statue of the Virgin. According to legend, the original was hidden from the Moors in the 8th century. More than 300 years later, it was re-discovered by Alfonso VI when part of the city wall fell away. On 9 November the statue is carried from the cathedral in solemn procession *(see p55)*.

6 Monasterio de la Encarnación

The convent was founded in 1611 by Margarita de Austria, wife of Felipe III, for daughters of the nobility. It was also the church of the Alcázar – a picture gallery linked the two buildings. Unfortunately, when the castle was destroyed by fire in 1734 the conflagration spread to the convent and many of its treasures were lost. A great deal remains however: 17th-century paintings by Ribera and Lucas Jordan; impressive sculptures, such as *Christ Recumbent* by Gregorio Fernández; embroidered vestments and liturgical gold and silverware. The guided tour takes in the cloister with its decoration of Talavera *azulejos*; the reliquary, where visitors are shown the phial containing the congealed blood of St Pantaleon; the carved stalls in the choir; and the church, designed by Ventura Rodríguez. ◈ *Plaza de la Encarnación 1 • Map K3 • Open 10am–2pm, 4–6:30pm Tue–Sat, 10am–3pm Sun & public hols • Closed 1 Jan, 6 Jan, Easter week, 1 May, 2 May, 15 May, 27 Jul, 9 Sep, 9 Nov, 24 Dec, 25 Dec, 31 Dec • Adm*

7 Teatro Real

The city's state-of-the-art opera house re-opened in 1998 after a lengthy and expensive restoration. There were so many delays in constructing the original theatre that the architect, Antonio López Aguado, was long dead before the official opening in 1850 on Queen Isabel II's birthday. Giuseppe Verdi wrote his opera *The Force of Destiny* for the Teatro Real in 1863 – he stayed at No.6 Plaza de Oriente. The dimensions of the restored opera house are impressive: the architects calculate that the backstage area is large enough to contain the Telefónica building on Gran Vía *(see p88)*. ◈ *Plaza Isabel II • Map K3 • Open for tours 10:30am–1pm Mon–Fri, 11am–1:30pm Sat & Sun • Closed 1 Jan, Aug, 25 Dec • Dis. access • Adm*

8 Catedral de la Almudena

There were plans to build a cathedral on the superb hilltop site in the 18th century, but it was not until 1879 that the Marqués de Cubas got the go-ahead for his ambitious design; even then, only the Romanesque-style crypt was built. The cathedral was finally completed In the 1980s by architect Fernando Chueca Goitia and opened by Pope John Paul II in 1993. The Gothic interior comes as a surprise, as the exterior is Neo-Classical to harmonize with the Palacio Real. The magnificent bronze doors were installed in October 2000. ◈ *Calle de Bailén • Map J4 • Open 9am–8pm daily • Dis. access • Free • Museum & dome: open 10am–2:30pm Mon–Sat; adm*

Plaza de Oriente

Plaza de España

Plaza de Oriente

9 The focal point of this beautiful square is the bronze equestrian statue of Felipe IV, moved here from the Buen Retiro palace in 1842. The sculptor Pietro Tacca took advice from Galileo on the modelling of the rearing horse – the figure of the king was based on sketches by Velázquez. The statues of Spanish rulers were intended for the balustrade of the Palacio Real but they did not meet with royal approval. ✎ *Map K3*

Plaza de España

10 A set piece of the Franco era, the huge square at the bottom of Gran Vía is dominated by Madrid's first skyscrapers. The Edificio España (Gran Vía 86) was design-ed by the brothers Julien and Joaquín Otamendi in 1953. Four years later, the same architects built the even taller Torre de Madrid (Plaza de España 18). The building is currently an office and residential apartment block. The monument at the centre of the square commemorates Miguel de Cervantes, author of *Don Quixote*. ✎ *Map K1*

A Day in Royal Madrid

Morning

🕐 Catch the first guided tour of the morning (10:30am) at the **Monasterio de las Descalzas Reales** *(see pp20–21)*. On leaving, cross Plaza San Martín to Calle de Hilera, then turn right onto Calle del Arenal. Follow this busy street to Plaza de Isabel II, the best place to admire Madrid's opera house, the **Teatro Real**. Follow Calle Felipe V alongside the theatre until you come to **Plaza de Oriente** and the **Palacio Real** *(see pp8–11)*. The palace is closed at least once a week for official functions but, if it is open, it is worth allocating an hour to looking around.

🍴 There are plenty of places to eat in the vicinity of Plaza de Oriente, for example the café of the same name *(see p101)*. A plaque on the wall nearby reminds visitors that this was once the treasury house where the artist Velázquez had his studio.

Afternoon

After the frantic activity of the morning, enjoy a restful afternoon in the **Casa de Campo** park *(see p50)*. If you didn't lunch at a café, a picnic may be a good idea. You could stock up at the Oriente's delicatessen, just round the corner at Calle Carlos III, 3 *(see p100)*. To get to Casa de Campo take the metro from Opera (on Plaza Isabel II) to Lago (line R to Principe Pío, then line 10). Here you can either enjoy a spot of peaceful sunbathing and people-watching, or take in one of the many attractions of the park.

Around Town – Downtown Madrid

Left **La Metralleta** Right **El Flamenco Vive**

Shops

1 La Metralleta
This large store specializes in second-hand records. Every taste and period is catered for and the staff are both helpful and knowledgeable. ◈ *Plaza de la Descalzas • Map M3*

2 Cántaro
A treasure trove for admirers of pottery and an excellent place to shop for gifts. Products from all over Spain at very reasonable prices. ◈ *Calle Flor Baja 8 • Map L1*

3 Antigua Casa Talavera
If you've been bowled over by the 18th-century Talavera ceramics in the Palacio Real, you'll find that the modern descendants of these craftsmen have not lost their touch. This outlet offers a wide range of hand-painted jugs, plates, mugs and more. ◈ *Calle de Isabel La Católica 2 • Map L2*

4 Manuel González Contreras
Good guitars don't come cheap and there's usually a long waiting list for a handmade instrument. This workshop may already have what you are looking for *(see p48)*. ◈ *Calle Mayor 80 • Map M4*

5 El Flamenco Vive
This family business specializes in all things Flamenco, from beautiful dresses to guitars, CDs, music and videos *(see p48)*. ◈ *Calle Conde de Lemos 7 • Map L4*

6 El Obrador del Café de Oriente
If you're planning a picnic in the Sabatini Gardens or further afield, the delicatessen of the Café del Oriente has everything you need, from fresh bread and filled rolls to cheeses, cooked meats and cakes. ◈ *Plaza de Oriente 2 • Map K4*

7 Ocho y Medio
Located in the centre of Madrid's main cinema district, this shop is a treasure house for film buffs, with books, posters, postcards and more. ◈ *Calle de Martín de los Heros 11 • Map J1*

8 Kukuxumusu
This design company started as three friends selling T-shirts on the streets of Pamplona during the 1989 Sanfermines fiesta. The bright graphics proved hugely popular, and Kukuxumusu now sells their products throughout Europe. ◈ *Calle Mayor 47 • Map M4*

9 El Riojano
Founded in 1855, this pretty, old-style *pastelería* caters for the Spanish royal family, no less. Shop here for seasonal Madrid specialities such as *tocino de cielo*. ◈ *Calle Mayor 10 • Map M4*

10 Toni Martín
Fans of country music, jazz and rock 'n' roll take note. This excellent outlet has a great selection of CDs and vinyl, new and second-hand. ◈ *Calle de Martín de los Heros 18 • Map J1*

Above **La Bola**

Price Categories

For a three-course meal for one with half a bottle of wine (or equivalent meal), taxes and extra charges.

€ under €25
€€ €25–€35
€€€ €35–€55
€€€€ €55–€70
€€€€€ over €70

Places to Eat and Drink

1 Chocolatería San Ginés
Head here after a night out for a traditional breakfast of *chocolate con churros*. ॐ *Pasadizo de S Ginés 5 • Map M4 • 91 365 6546 • Open 9–7am daily • €*

2 Taberna del Alabardero
Snack on *jamón Ibérico* or *croquetas* in the *tapas* bar or eat Basque food in the adjoining restaurant. ॐ *Calle de Felipe V 6 • Map K3 • 91 547 2577 • Open noon–1am daily • €€€*

3 Casa Ciriaco
Try classic dishes like the dessert *bizcocho borracho* (sponge cake soaked in wine and syrup). ॐ *Calle Mayor 84 • Map M3 • 91 548 0620 • Closed Wed, Aug • €€*

4 Café de Oriente
An elegant café with velvet seats, stucco ceiling and summer terrace. ॐ *Plaza de Oriente 2 • Map K3 • 91 541 3974 • €€€*

5 Entre Suspiro y Suspiro
Tasty Mexican dishes include "devil salad" with prawns, mango, coriander and chicken in chocolate sauce *(mole)*. ॐ *Calle de Caños del Peral 3 • Map L3 • 91 542 0644 • Closed Sat L, 22 Dec, 25 Dec • €€€*

6 La Bola
Cocido (various meats cooked in a rich broth) is the highlight at this 19th-century restaurant. ॐ *Calle de la Bola 5 • Map L2 • 91 547 6930 • Closed Sun D, 24 Dec, 25 Dec • No credit cards • €€*

7 La Vaca Argentina
One of a chain of steak houses specializing in grilled beef straight from the pampas. Can be noisy. ॐ *Calle de Caños de Peral 2 • Map L3 • 91 541 3318 • €€€*

8 El Cangrejero
This bar has a good choice of seafood *tapas*. Mahou beer originally came from the factory next door. ॐ *Calle de Amaniel 25 • Map C2 • 91 548 3935 • Closed Sun D, Wed • No credit cards • €*

9 Entrevinos
The wine list is excellent here. Speciality snacks include *habas* (salted broad beans) with *jamón Ibérico*. ॐ *Calle de Ferraz 36 • Map J1 • 91 548 3114 • Closed 1 Jan, 6 Jan, Aug, 24 Dec, 25 Dec, 31 Dec • €€*

10 Mercado de San Miguel
This renovated early 20th-century market is where the best shops have stalls, selling cheese, ham, sushi, foie gras and pastries. Weekends can be very crowded. ॐ *Plaza de San Miguel • Map L5 • 91 542 4936 • Open daily 10am–midnight (to 2am Thu–Sat) • €*

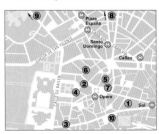

Note: Unless otherwise stated, all restaurants accept credit cards and serve vegetarian meals

Left **Museo de los Orígenes Casa de San Isidro** Right **Plaza Mayor**

Old Madrid

IN THE 17TH CENTURY THE FOCUS OF THE RAPIDLY GROWING CITY *shifted from the medieval centre, around Plaza de la Paja, to Plaza Mayor. Part market, part meeting place, this magnificent square was, above all, a place of spectacle and popular entertainment. The names of the playwrights of Spain's Golden Age are still commemorated in the streets around Calle de las Huertas, where many of them lived. There were no permanent theatres in those days; instead, makeshift stages were erected in courtyards. Over time the houses deteriorated into slums and teeming tenements. The parishes to the south of Plaza Mayor were known as the barrios bajas (low districts), because they were low-lying and were home to Madrid's labouring classes. Mingling with the slaughterhouse workers and tanners of the Rastro were market traders, builders, innkeepers, horse-dealers and even the criminal underclass.*

🔟 Sights

1. Plaza Mayor
2. El Rastro
3. Plaza de la Villa
4. Museo de los Orígenes Casa de San Isidro
5. Real Basílica de San Francisco el Grande
6. Lavapiés
7. La Latina
8. Casa-Museo de Lope de Vega
9. Plaza de Santa Ana
10. Casa de la Villa

Mural, Lavapiés

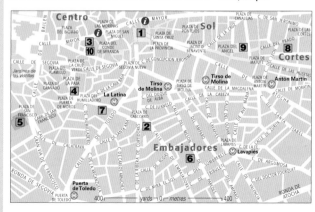

102

1 Plaza Mayor
The heart of Old Madrid is this vast square, surrounded by arcaded buildings, now home to tourist shops *(see pp18–19)*.

2 El Rastro
You can easily lose a day wandering around the quirky stalls of the city's flea market and watching the bustling world go by in the many bars and cafés *(see pp22–3)*.

3 Plaza de la Villa
This historic square off Calle Mayor has been the centre of local government since medieval times. Opposite the Casa de la Villa *(see p105)* is the Casa y Torre de los Lujanes, Madrid's oldest civil building (15th century). In the centre of the square is a statue of Alvaro de Bazán, the Spanish admiral who defeated the Turks at Lepanto in 1571 *(see p40)*. Erected in the late 19th century, it is by sculptor Mariano Benlliure. The palace on the south side is the Casa de Cisneros (1537), built for one of Spain's most powerful families. Ⓢ *Map K5*

4 Museo de los Orígenes Casa de San Isidro
The museum is housed in an attractive 16th-century palace which once belonged to the Counts of Paredes. The original Renaissance courtyard is best viewed from the first floor where archaeological finds from the Madrid region are exhibited, including a Roman mosaic floor from the 4th century. Downstairs, the highlights include wooden models of the city and its royal palaces as they would have appeared in the 17th century, a short film bringing to life Francisco Ricci's painting of the 1680 *auto-de-fé (see p19)* and the San

Real Basílica de San Francisco el Grande

Isidro chapel built near the spot where the saint is said to have died. Ⓢ *Plaza de S Andrés 2 • Map K6 • Open 9:30am–8pm Tue–Fri, 10am–2pm Sat & Sun (Aug: 9am–2:30pm Tue–Sun) • Closed public hols • Free*

5 Real Basílica de San Francisco el Grande
Legend has it that this magnificent basílica occupies the site of a monastery founded by St Francis of Assisi in the 13th century. Work on the present building was completed in 1784 under the supervision of Francesco Sabatini. The focal point of the unusual circular design is the stupendous dome, 58 m (190 ft) high and 33 m (110 ft) in diameter. After 30 years of restoration, the 19th-century ceiling frescos, painted by leading artists, are now revealed in their original glory. Take the guided tour to be shown other treasures, including paintings by Zurbarán and Goya and the Gothic choir. Ⓢ *Calle San Buenaventura • Map B5 • Open 11am–12:30pm, 4–6:30pm Tue–Fri, 11am–1:30pm Sat; Aug: 11am–12:30pm, 5–7:30pm Tue–Sun • Adm*

San Isidro

When the future patron saint of Madrid died around 1170 he was buried in a pauper's grave. But, in the 17th century, an unseemly rivalry developed between the clergy of San Andrés and the Capilla de San Isidro over the custody of his mortal remains. The wrangle dragged on until the 18th century when the body of the saint was interred in the new Catedral de San Isidro where it has remained ever since.

Lavapiés

6 This colourful working-class neighbourhood has a cosmopolitan feel, thanks to its ethnic mix of Moroccans, Indians, Turks and Chinese. The narrow streets sloping towards the river from Plaza Tirso de Molina are full of shops selling everything from cheap clothes and leather handbags to tea and spices. Check out the traditional bars, such as Taberna Antonio Sánchez *(see p67)*. Per-formances of the traditional light opera known as *zarzuela* are given outdoors in La Corrala on Calle Mesón de Paredes 64 in the summer. Map D6

La Latina

7 Historic La Latina really comes alive on Sundays when the trendy bars of Cava Baja, Calle de Don Pedro and Plaza de los Carros are frequented by pop singers, actors and TV stars.

Lavapiés district

Façade, La Latina

Plaza de la Paja – the main square of medieval Madrid – takes its name from the straw which was sold here by villagers from the across the River Manzanares. Nowadays it's much quieter and a nice place to rest one's legs. The two churches of San Andrés and San Pedro el Viejo have been restored. Their history and that of the area as a whole is admirably explained in the Museo de San Isidro *(see p103)*. Map L6

Casa-Museo de Lope de Vega

8 The greatest dramatist of Spain's Golden Age lived in this roomy, two-storey brick house from 1610 until his death in 1635. Lope de Vega started writing at the age of 12 and his tally of 1,500 plays (not counting poetry, novels and devotional works) has never been beaten. He became a priest after the death of his second wife in 1614, but that didn't stop his compulsive philandering which led to more than one run-in with the law. To tour the restored house with its heavy wooden shutters, creaking staircases and beamed ceilings is to step back in time. You get to see the author's bedroom, and the book-lined study where he wrote many of his plays. The women of the house gathered in the adjoining embroidery room – the heavy wall-hangings were to keep out the cold. Other evocative details include a cloak, sword and belt discarded by one of Lope's friends in the guest bedroom. ◈ *Calle de Cervantes 11 • Map R5 • Open for tours in English 10am–3pm Tue–Sun (call 91 429 9216 to book in advance) • Closed public hols • Free*

Plaza de Santa Ana
The streets around this well-known square boast the greatest concentration of *tapas* bars in the city and it's often still buzzing at 4am. The stylish hotel ME Madrid dominates the square, and there is an amazing view from its penthouse bar of the Teatro Español opposite. ◈ *Map P5*

Casa de la Villa
For hundreds of years Madrid's town council met in the church of San Salvador (since demolished) but in 1644 they were given a new home. The Town Hall was completed 50 years later. Its austere brick and granite façade, steepled towers and ornamental portals are typical of the architectural style favoured by the Habsburgs. Juan de Villanueva added the balcony overlooking Calle Mayor so that Queen María Luisa could watch the annual Corpus Christi procession. Highlights of the tour include the gala staircase, hung with tapestries designed by Rubens; the reception hall with its painted ceiling and chandelier; the 16th-century silver mons-trance carried in the Corpus Christi procession; the courtyard with stained-glass ceiling; and the debating chamber with frescoes by Antonio Palomino. ◈ *Plaza de la Villa 5 • Map K5 • Open for guided tour 5pm Mon • Free*

A Morning Walk Around Old Madrid

Begin the morning at **Plaza de la Villa** *(see p103)* with its handsome 16th- and 17th-century palaces. Take the busy Calle Mayor as far as Calle de Felipe III, then turn into **Plaza Mayor** *(see pp18–19)*. Cross this magnificent square diagonally, leaving by the ancient Calle Toledo, once the main exit south from the city. On the way look out for the **Hernanz** rope store *(see p109)* and other reminders that this was once an artisans' quarter. Looming on the left is the Baroque **Colegiata de San Isidro** *(see p108)*. Continue to La Latina metro.

Turn and follow Plaza de la Cebada, past the modern covered market. Turn right into Plaza del Humilladero and cross this square to the adjoining Plaza de San Andrés and its huge domed church. Straight ahead is a 16th-century palace, now the **Museo de los Orígenes Casa de San Isidro** *(see p103)*. Follow the path round the back of the church into Costanilla de San Andrés, a narrow street which opens onto the historic **Plaza de la Paja**, a good area for bars and restaurants. On the corner of Calle de Alfonso VI is the Colegio de San Ildefonso whose students chant the results of the Christmas National Lottery in a distinctive sing-song.

By now you'll probably be ready for lunch. Vegetarians will be tempted by El Estragón *(Plaza de la Paja 10)*; another good choice is the Basque Taberna Bilbao *(Calle Costinilla de San Andrés 8)*.

Following pages **Parque del Retiro** (see pp32–3)

Left **Muralla Árabe** Right **Teatro Español**

Top 10 Best of the Rest

Ateneo de Madrid
One of Madrid's great cultural institutions, the Ateneo was founded in 1835 to promote the arts and sciences. The building contains a library of half a million volumes. ⊗ *Calle del Prado 21 • Map R5 • Guided tours available 10am–1pm Mon–Fri (advance booking necessary) • Adm*

Colegiata de San Isidro
This imposing church was built in 1622 by the Jesuits. In 1768 the remains of Madrid's patron saint, San Isidro, were interred here. ⊗ *Calle de Toledo 37–9 • Map M6 • Open for services • Free*

Palacio de Santa Cruz
This 17th-century palace has lovely spired towers and interior courtyards. It was originally used as the city prison, but now houses the Ministry of Foreign Affairs. ⊗ *Plaza de la Provincia • Map M5*

Teatro Español
Spain's National Theatre began as an open courtyard with a wooden platform for a stage. Look for the medallions depicting the country's best-known dramatists above the entrance. ⊗ *Calle del Príncipe 25 • Map Q5*

Teatro Clásico
The Comedy Theatre stages classical plays, despite its name. The lovely façade dates from 1874; the auditorium was restored in the 1990s. ⊗ *Calle del Príncipe 14 • Map Q5*

Calle de las Huertas
The name refers to the orchards that flourished here in the 17th century. Today the street is better known for its nightlife. ⊗ *Map Q5*

Muralla Árabe
Remains of the medieval defences are best seen from Parque Emir Mohammad I. The original section is 9th-century. ⊗ *Cuesta de la Vega • Map J5*

Cervecería Alemana
This popular beer and *tapas* bar was founded in 1904 and is still going strong (see p65). ⊗ *Plaza de Sta Ana 6 • Map P5 • Closed Tue, Aug*

Plaza de Tirso de Molina
Laid out in the 1840s, this square commemorates the creator of the infamous seducer, Don Juan. ⊗ *Map N6*

Cine Doré
The cinematograph was introduced to a Madrid audience from a booth on the site of what is now, fittingly, the cinema house Cine Doré (see p56). ⊗ *Calle de Sta Isabel 3 • Map Q6 • Closed Mon*

Left **Casa Hernanz** Right **Seseña**

⏁⏁⏁ Specialist Shops

Casa Hernanz
One of a number of intriguing shops on Calle de Toledo, Casa Hernanz specializes in items made of rope, such as espadrilles, baskets and mats.
◈ *Calle de Toledo 18–20 • Map M5*

Tea Shop
You will find an exquisite selection of teas from around the world in this delightful shop. Be sure to try the aromatic and exotic infusions such as "Andalusian Garden" or "La Siesta". ◈ *Calle Mayor 12 • Map M4*

Santería la Milagrosa
Fascinating emporium near Sol dealing in things spiritual – everything from amulets and birth charts to tarot cards, books on white magic and icons. ◈ *Calle de Espoz y Mina 5 • Map P4*

Biocentro
Health food shop with a good selection of natural products, mainly food (including vacuum-packed 100 per cent vegeburgers) and cosmetics.
◈ *Calle de Espoz y Mina 3 • Map P4*

Casa Mira
Founded in 1842 by Luis Mira, who knew how to cater for the famous Spanish sweet tooth, this *confitería* (confectioner) is best known for its *turrón* (Christmas nougat); also marzipan, chocolate and *pestiños* (honey-coated pastries). ◈ *Carrera de S Jerónimo 30 • Map P4*

La Violeta
This quaint store, founded more than a century ago, sells its own brand of sugared violets, plus a small range of *marrons glacés*, pralines and other sweets.
◈ *Plaza de Canalejas 6 • Map Q4*

Europa 20
This family-run home furnishings store stocks a range of stylish modern furniture including sofas, lighting and accessories. ◈ *Carrera de San Jerónimo 32 • Map E4*

Nike
A four-floor emporium of sport, Nike contains the latest collections of sports clothing and equipment – everything you could ever need to get fit.
◈ *Calle Gran Via 38 • Map D3*

Jamones Julian Becerro
This shop offers a variety of Iberian pork products from Salamanca, such as ham and sausages. Acorn ham (*jamón de bellota*) is considered to be the best. Cheese, foie gras and liquor are also sold. ◈ *Cava Baja 41 • Map L6*

Seseña
Would-be matadors should first make their way here to be kitted out with the traditional Spanish cape. Set up in 1901, this is still a family-run business where each cape is produced individually. Be warned, they don't come cheaply *(see p48)*.
◈ *Calle de la Cruz 23 • Map P4*

For more specialist shops in Madrid **See pp48–9**

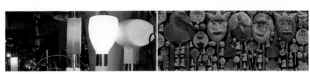

Left **El Transformista** Right **Caramelos Paco**

Top 10 Shops in La Latina

Caramelos Paco
The display windows of this famous sweet emporium are ablaze with colour. Some of the flavours – rice pudding, for example – sound less appealing than others. Sugar-free sweets for diabetics. ❧ *Calle de Toledo 55 • Map M5*

El Transformista
Delve into this Aladdin's cave for antique and second-hand furniture – everything from old mirrors and table lamps to painted plates and plastic chairs. ❧ *Calle de Mira el Río Baja 18 • Map C6*

Casa Vega
This Aladdin's cave sells an unusual array of goods from saddles to espadrilles. The inside seems to have changed little since it opened in 1860. ❧ *Calle Toledo 57 • Map C5*

Fotocasión
Stocks just about everything the photographer might need – cameras, new and second-hand, film, camera cases, tripods and other specialist equipment. Also sells binoculars. ❧ *Ribera de Curtidores 22 • Map C6*

Mercado de la Cebada
If you want artisanal hams and cheeses but prefer not to go to a tourist spot, try this market. It is popular with locals and many of its vendors supply some of Madrid's best restaurants. ❧ *Plaza Cebada 15 • Map L6*

La Tienda de las Hamacas
A shop dedicated to the fine art of making hammocks, La Tienda de las Hamacas sells every kind of hammock for home or garden. Particularly special are the handmade Mayan styles. ❧ *Calle Miguel Servet 6 • Map D6*

María José Fermín
Wrought-iron enthusiasts, look no further. This family business deals in everything from coal scuttles and fire-guards to bellows, weather vanes and milk churns. ❧ *Ribera de Curtidores 2 • Map C6*

La Studio
Rifle through an amazing range of antiques and *objets d'art* from retro sofas and art deco lamps to original oil paintings and gilded looking glasses. ❧ *Calle Arganzuela 18 • Map C6*

Nuevas Galerías
Shop here for prints, lithographs, repro-ceramics and antiques. Souvenir hunters should make a bee-line for Albarrelo and Mercedes Cabeza de Vaca. ❧ *Ribera de Curtidores 12 • Map C6*

Marihuana Bronca Total
This goth's paradise deals in spiked arm bands, studded belts and leather gear, but is also hot on T-shirts – Superman, Che Guevara, Metallica, Jimi Hendrix, take your pick. ❧ *Plaza Cascorro 6 • Map C6*

Left **La Negra Tomasa** Centre **Casa PATAS** Right **Café Central**

TOP 10 Nights Out

1 Casa PATAS
Aficionados rate this attractive venue as the best place for traditional Spanish Flamenco acts *(see p60)*. ◊ Calle de Cañizares 10 • Map P6

2 Viva Madrid
Worth seeing for the decorative tiles alone, this *tapas* bar near Huertas really gets going after 10pm and is a popular hang-out with the young crowd. In the summer you may need to cool off on the terrace. Full to bursting at weekends. ◊ Calle Manuel Fernández y González 7 • Map P6

3 Café Central
Sophisticated jazz lovers home in on this Art Deco café at the top of Huertas. There's a small admission charge, depending on the artists *(see p60)*. ◊ Plaza del Ángel 10 • Map P5

4 Populart
Eclectic live music nightly – anything from blues or jazz to Celtic – and beer on tap. No cover charge, but be warned that there's a steep mark-up on drinks *(see p60)*. ◊ Calle de las Huertas 22 • Map Q5

5 La Negra Tomasa
The live salsa music, played Thursdays to Saturdays inclusive, is the main draw of this noisy Cuban restaurant *(see p60)*. ◊ Corner of Calle de Espoz y Mina, Cádiz 9 • Map P4

6 Cool
Dance until 6am at this fashionable club to the sounds of DJs or live music in a range of different styles (Thu–Sun). ◊ Calle Isabel la Católica 6 • Map L2

7 Teatro Circo Price
This theatre is named after an Irish horse tamer called Thomas Price who came to Madrid in the 19th century and set up a circus. It is now the place to see avant-garde performances in Madrid. ◊ Ronda de Atocha 35 • Map E6

8 La Boca del Lobo
This lively and hip cellar venue (the name means "the jaws of the wolf") has a great atmosphere. They dance to anything here – funk, soul, rock 'n' roll, you name it. ◊ Calle de Echegaray 11 • Map Q5

9 Villa Rosa
On a corner of buzzing Plaza de Santa Ana *(see p105)*, this interestingly tiled restaurant offers entertaining flamenco tableaux with dinner from 9pm to 3am *(see p61)*. ◊ Plaza de Santa Ana 15 • Map P5

10 Palacio de Gaviria
This ornate 19th-century palace is the city's most unusual club. There are several bars, and a huge ballroom, which still has its original decor. Listen to live music or join the crowds on the dance floor. ◊ Calle Arenal 9 • Map N4

Left **La Trucha** Right **Casa Alberto**

Places to Eat and Drink

1 La Trucha
Show-business types from the Teatro Español next door patronize this bar-restaurant, a great place to sample *tapas* in a relaxed ambience. Try *rabo de toro* (bull's tail). ◐ Calle de Núñez de Arce 6 • Map Q5 • 91 532 0890 • Closed Sun & Mon, Aug • €

2 Casa Alberto
This historic tavern serving traditional *madrileño* cooking is where the author Cervantes wrote part of *Don Quixote*. Wood panelling gives it a warm atmosphere. Vermouth is dispensed on draught from an antique pump. ◐ Calle de las Huertas 18 • Map Q5 • 91 429 9356 • Closed Sun D, Mon, Aug • €€

3 Casa Lucas
There is a good choice of wines and large *tapas* for sharing on offer here. ◐ Cava Baja 30 • Map L6 • 91 365 0804 • Closed Wed L • €€

4 Casa González
This popular wine bar is housed in a converted 1930s deli. There is a huge selection of wines, *empanadas* (pies) and ice creams. ◐ Calle León 12 • Map Q5 • 91 429 5618 • Closed Sun & Mon • €€

5 Casa Lucio
It's worth splashing out on a meal in this restaurant renowned for its roasts. Booking ahead is essential. ◐ Calle de la Cava Baja 35 • Map L6 • 91 365 8217 • Closed Sat L, Aug • €€€€

6 Taberna de Antonio Sánchez
The ambience is reason enough for visiting this traditional inn. *Tapas* include black pudding with raisins *(see p67)*. ◐ Calle de Mesón de Paredes 13 • Map N6 • 91 539 7826 • Closed Sun D, Mon, 15–31 Aug • €

7 The Penthouse
This stylish rooftop terrace has two indoor bars and Bedouin-style tents for relaxing. ◐ Hotel ME Madrid, Plaza Santa Ana 14 • Map P5 • 90 214 4440 • €€€€

8 La Venencia
Sherry is the speciality of this small, lively bar that serves simple *tapas* dishes. ◐ Calle de Echegaray 7 • Map Q5 • 91 429 7313 • €

9 Alhambra
Enjoy good Spanish wine and Iberian ham at this atmospheric *tapas* bar. It is crowded at weekends *(see p65)*. ◐ Calle de la Victoria 9 • Map P4 • 91 521 0708 • €

10 Taberna Almendro 13
This tastefully decorated *tapas* restaurant has an Andalusian theme. ◐ Calle del Almendro 13 • Map L6 • 91 365 4252 • €

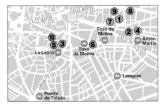

Above **Botín**

Price Categories

For a three-course meal for one with half a bottle of wine (or equivalent meal), taxes and extra charges.	**€** under €25
	€€ €25–€35
	€€€ €35–€55
	€€€€ €55–€70
	€€€€€ over €70

🔟 Traditional Restaurants and Bars

1 La Posada de la Villa
This attractive inn dates back to 1642. Traditional Castilian cooking is served, especially roasts. ✆ Calle de la Cava Baja 9 • Map L6 • 91 366 1860 • Closed Sun D, Aug • €€€ • Dis. access

2 Botín
American writer Ernest Hemingway was a fan of this restaurant. His favourite dish, roast suckling pig, is still a house speciality (see p68). ✆ Calle de la Cuchilleros 17 • Map M5 • 91 366 4217 • €€€€

3 La Torre del Oro
Tapas are free when you buy a drink at this outrageous Andalusian bar decorated with mounted bull heads, videos of bullfights and gory pictures. ✆ Plaza Mayor 26 • Map L4 • 91 366 5016 • Closed Jan • €

4 La Casa del Abuelo
This tapas bar par excellence was founded in 1906 and is still going strong. The speciality of the house is prawns (see p66). ✆ Calle de la Victoria 12 • Map P4 • 91 000 0133 • €

5 Taberna Oliveros
Dating back to 1857, this taberna has an old-world charm. It's worth trying their main speciality, cocido madrileño – a stew made from chick peas, tripe and fried bacalao (see p62). ✆ Calle San Millán • Map D6 • 91 354 6252 • Closed Sun D, Mon, Jul, Aug • €

6 Aloque
A fine wine list accompanies delicious raciones (large tapas). ✆ Calle Torrecilla del Leal 20 • Map Q5 • 91 528 3662 • Closed Mon • €€

7 El Viajero
The third-floor terrace is very popular during the evening and weekend, as is the restaurant below. ✆ Plaza de la Cebada 11 • Map L6 • 91 366 9064 • Closed Mon, public hols • €€

8 Taberna Maceiras
Chaotic and noisy, this restaurant is still well worth a visit for the great seafood, almond cake and wines. ✆ Huertas 66 • Map R6 • 91 429 5818 • Closed Tue L • €€€

9 Arrocería Gala
The glass-roofed terrace is the main attraction of this restaurant specializing in rice-based dishes. ✆ Calle Moratín 22 • Map R6 • 91 429 2562 • Closed Mon • €€

10 Asador Arizmendi
Meat and fish dishes are grilled over charcoal at this classic asador (see p69). ✆ Plaza de Tirso de Molina 7 • Map N6 • 91 429 5030 • Closed Sun D, Easter, Aug (15 days) • €€€

Left **Calle de Fuencarral** Right **Palacio Longoría**

Chueca and Malasaña

TWO OF MADRID'S MOST LIVELY *BARRIOS* lie just off the Gran Vía. Chueca was originally home to the city's blacksmiths and tile-makers. Run-down for many years, it has enjoyed a renaissance after being adopted by Madrid's gay community – the area puts on its glad rags every summer for the Gay Pride celebrations. The 19th-century buildings around Plaza de Chueca have been given a new lease of life as trendy bars and restaurants. Neighbouring Malasaña was the focus of resistance against the French in 1808. Like Chueca, it became rather seedy, but is now a mainstay of Madrid nightlife.

🔟 Sights

1. Casa de las Siete Chimeneas
2. Museo del Romanticismo
3. Museo de Historia
4. Palacio Longoría
5. Iglesia de San Antonio de los Alemanes
6. Calle de Fuencarral
7. Plaza del Dos de Mayo
8. Iglesia San Plácido
9. Palacio de Justicia (Tribunal Supremo)
10. Iglesia de Santa Bárbara

Museo Romántico

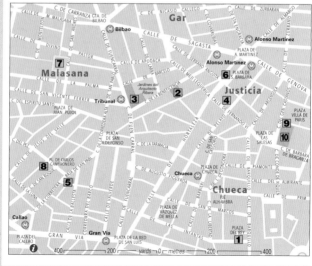

Share your travel recommendations on traveldk.com

1 Casa de las Siete Chimeneas

The "house of the seven chimneys" dates from around 1570 and is one of the best-preserved examples of domestic architecture in Madrid. The building is said to be haunted by a former lover of Felipe II – not as far-fetched as it sounds, as a female skeleton was uncovered here at the end of the 19th century. The house later belonged to Carlos III's chief minister, the Marqués de Esquilache, whose attempts to outlaw the traditional gentleman's cape and broad-brimmed hat, on the grounds that rogues used one to conceal weapons and the other to hide their faces, provoked a riot and his dismissal. ◈ Calle Infantas 31 • Map F3 • Closed to the public

2 Museo del Romanticismo

This evocative museum recreates the Madrid of the Romantic era (c.1820–60), with rooms furnished in the style of the period. The real attraction lies in the ephemera: fans, figurines, dolls, old photograph albums, cigar cases, visiting cards and the like. Among the paintings is a magnificent Goya in the chapel and a portrait of the Marqués de Vega-Inclán, whose personal possessions form the basis of the collection. By common consent, the archetypal Spanish Romantic was Mariano José de Larra, a journalist with a caustic pen, who shot himself in 1837 after his lover ran off with another man. The pistol is one of the museum's prized exhibits. ◈ Calle de S Mateo 13 • Map E2 • Open 9:30am–8:30pm Tue–Sat (Nov–Apr: 9:30am–6:30pm), 10am–3pm Sun & public hols • Closed Mon, 1 & 6 Jan, 1 May, 24 Dec, 25 Dec, 31 Dec • Adm (free Sat after 2pm)

Façade, Museo de Historia

3 Museo de Historia

Once a poorhouse, this museum traces the history of Madrid from the earliest times to the present day. Prize exhibits include mosaic fragments from a local Roman villa, pottery from the time of the Muslim occupation, a bust of Felipe II, and Goya's Allegory of the City of Madrid (Dos de Mayo). The star attraction is a wooden model of the city constructed in 1830 by León Gil de Palacio. As you leave, take a look at the elaborate Baroque portal, dating from the 1720s. ◈ Calle de Fuencarral 78 • Map E2 • Open 9:30am–8pm Tue–Fri, 10am–2pm Sat & Sun • Closed Mon & public hols • Free

4 Palacio Longoria

The finest example of Art Nouveau architecture in Madrid was created for the banker Javier González Longoria in 1902. The architect was José Grases Riera, a disciple of Antoni Gaudí. Magnificently restored in the 1990s, the walls, windows and balconies are covered with luxuriant decoration suggesting plants, flowers and tree roots (see p46). ◈ Calle de Fernando VI, 4 • Map E2 • Closed to public

5 Iglesia de San Antonio de los Alemanes

The entire surface area of this magnificent domed church is covered with 17th-century frescoes depicting scenes from the life of St Anthony of Padua. The congregation included the sick and indigent residents of the adjoining hospice, who were allocated a daily ration of bread and boiled eggs. (The church still has a soup kitchen). ◈ *Corredera Baja de S Pablo 16 • Map N1 • Open for services • Free*

6 Calle de Fuencarral

This narrow, partly pedestrianized street, is worth negotiating for its original and offbeat shops. Outlets include Spanish designer Adolfo Domínguez's U (No. 5), which sells impeccably designed modern clothes. For necklaces and bracelets in silver and leather, there is One of 50 (No. 25), while Hakei (No. 35) has a large selection of high-quality leather shoes, bags and belts. Cafés Pozo (No. 53) offers its own blends of coffee and tea, while Retoque (No. 47), founded in 1920, goes in for picture frames and modern art posters. ◈ *Map D2*

Manuela Malasaña

The seamstress, who became a national heroine following the 1808 uprising, was still a teenager on that fateful day in May, when, so the story goes, she was approached by a couple of French soldiers. Despite her protestations, they insisted on conducting a body search, provoking her to stab at them with a pair of dressmaking scissors. They shot her dead, but her memory lives on in the district which now bears her name.

Iglesia San Plácido

7 Plaza del Dos de Mayo

This square in the heart of Malasaña commemorates the leaders of the insurrection of May 1808, Luis Daoíz and Pedro Velarde, who are buried in the Plaza de Lealtad *(see p73)*. The site was chosen because, in those days, this was the artillery barracks of the Monteleón Palace, the main focus of resistance to the French. The brick arch now sheltering a sculpture of the two heroes was the entrance to the building. In the 1990s the square was taken over by underage drinkers who gathered here at weekends for binges known as *botellón*. Though it has now been reclaimed by local residents, it is best avoided at night. ◈ *Map D2*

8 Iglesia San Plácido

Founded in 1622 by Don Jerónimo de Villanueva, a Madrid nobleman, the early history of this convent was darkened by scandal. Rumours of sexual misconduct among the novices led to an investigation by the Inquisition which implicated the chaplain, the abbess and the Don himself. It was even rumoured that Felipe IV made nocturnal visits to the convent via a passageway under the street.

Today the main attraction is the splendid Baroque church (1655). The retable over the altar contains a magnificent *Annunciation* by Claudio Coello. ◈ *Calle S Roque 9 • Map N1 • Open for services • Free*

9 Palacio de Justicia (Palace of Justice)
Designed by Francisco Carlier and Francisco Moradillo and constructed between 1750 and 1757, the building served as a convent until 1870. The conversion into the Palace of Justice was carried out by architect Antonio Ruiz de Salces, but its present appearance is due to the restoration work that followed a fire in 1915. ◈ *Plaza Villa de Paris • Map F2 • Closed to public*

10 Iglesia de Santa Bárbara
The monastery of the Royal Salesians was founded by the wife of Fernando VI, as a refuge from her overbearing mother-in-law should the king die before her (in fact, she died first). You can still see the lavish Baroque church (1750), sculptures and decorative details on the façade and the tombs of Fernando VI and his wife by Francesco Gutiérrez. ◈ *Calle de General Castaños 2 • Map F3 • Open for services • Free*

Iglesia de Santa Bárbara

An Evening Shop and Bar Crawl

Start this evening walk around 5pm when the shops re-open after the *siesta*. Take the metro to Chueca, emerging on Plaza de Chueca, heart of Madrid's gay quarter. Look out for **Taberna del Angel Sierra**, a traditional tiled bar with zinc counter and painted ceiling *(see p123)*. From here take Calle de Gravina into Calle del Almirante. These streets are the wealthy shopper's paradise, with designer names jockeying for position on both sides. Turn onto Calle de la Libertad, then take a right at Calle de Augusto Figueroa, famous for shoes sold at knock-down prices.

Cross Calle de Hortaleza and continue to **Calle de Fuencarral**. Turn right here, heading for the **Museo de Historia** *(see p115)* and spend a few minutes admiring its excellent Baroque façade. Further on turn left into Calle Manuela Malasaña.

Trendy Malasaña is full of enticing restaurants and *tapas* bars so make a mental note of anywhere that takes your fancy for later. Walk past **Molly Malone's Pub** at Calle Malasaña No. 11, then cross **Plaza del Dos de Mayo**. If you've worked up a thirst, then the handy bistro-bar at No. 10 called **Nina Madrid** might fit the bill. Walk along Calle de San Andrés to Calle de San Vicente Ferrer. Return for a bite to eat at your chosen *tapas* bar, then head for home on Calle de San Vicente Ferrer for the metro at Tribunal, or head off for a night on the tiles.

Following pages **Neptune Fountain on Paseo del Prado**

Left **Alcoba** Right **Hand**

10 Fashion Shops

1 Camper
For internationally acclaimed, comfortable and casual footwear, head to Camper, which stocks a selection of shoes produced in Mallorca. ✆ *Calle Fuencarral 42 (Cnr Augusto Figueroa) • Map P1*

2 Hand
The acronym for "have a nice day", Hand is french-run and specializes in beautiful, well-made clothes from French, Danish and English designers. ✆ *Calle Hortaleza 26 • Map Q2*

3 Piamonte
At Piamonte you can find handbags for any kind of special occasion, and have them made to order. There's also a similarly striking range of scarves, belts and jewellery. ✆ *Calle de Piamonte 16 • Map F3*

4 Momo
This lovely boutique stocks everything from casual outfits, to smarter, evening ensembles from a range of worldwide designers. ✆ *Calle Almirante 8 • Map F3*

5 Custo Barcelona
Set up by Custo and David Dalmau in the early 1980s, this fashion house is inspired by the colours and patterns of California. The shop has plenty of pretty dresses and coats for women, while style-conscious men will love the graphic T-shirts and tailored jackets ✆ *Calle de Fuencarral 29 • Map P2*

6 L'Habilleur
At l'Habilleur you can pick up last season's designer clothes at a fraction of the original prices. ✆ *Plaza de Chueca 8 • Map E3*

7 Maje
Cool French fashion is available at Maje. Catering for stylish ladies, there is a huge variety of smart dresses, tops, trousers and knitwear to browse through. The shop also stocks some shoes. ✆ *Calle Fuencarral 10 • Map F3*

8 Jesús del Pozo
One of the most respected Spanish designers, del Pozo first broke away from the mainstream in the 1970s and has never looked back. Sophisticated women's fashions and *prêt-à-porter*; also sells his own brand of perfume. ✆ *Calle del Almirante 9 • Map F3*

9 Farina & Almuzara
Beautiful hand-crafted gems are made on the premises from natural stones such as amber and amethyst. There is a range of styles, and you can design your own piece if you wish. ✆ *Calle de Conde de Xiquena 12 • Map E4*

10 Alcoba
This small outlet sells a lovely range of glitzy evening wear, with sequinned bags, scarves and other accessories. It also has candles, picture frames and costume jewellery. ✆ *Calle de Argensola 2 • Map E3*

Left **Patrimonio Comunal Olivarero** Right **Alice in Wonderland**

🔟 Specialist Shops

1 Patrimonio Comunal Olivarero
Spain produces more olive oil than any other country, and this supplier stocks the finest Extra Virgin. Also look for the DO *(denominación de origen)* quality control on the label *(see p48)*. ✆ *Calle de Mejía Lequerica 1 • Map E2*

2 Casa Crespo 1863
This charming sandal shop was established in 1863. It sells traditional espadrilles, hand woven and sewn by artisans from the La Rioja region of Spain. The shop is also patronized by Spanish royalty. ✆ *Calle Divino Pastor 29 • Map D2*

3 Reserva y Cata
Take care not to overlook this basement wine merchants with its excellent selection of Spanish wines and liqueurs. Tastings are also on offer. ✆ *Calle de Conde de Xiquena 13 • Map F3*

4 Expresión Negra
Selling African arts and crafts, this shop has woven baskets, rugs and colourful patchwork quilts. There are also recycled drink cans, ingeniously transformed into CD racks, boxes, briefcases and other useful items. ✆ *Calle de Piamonte 15 • Map F3*

5 Kantharos
Stylish gifts at this shop include pocket- as well as wrist-watches, key rings, jewellery, ink wells, etc. ✆ *Divino Pastor 6 • Map E3*

6 La Mona Checa
Packed with a great selection of retro clothes and accessories, this shop also has an area for art displays and a collection of cameras. ✆ *Calle Velarde 2 • Map D2*

7 Almirante 23
If it's collectable, they collect it – postcards, perfume containers, tobacco tins, cameras, sunglasses, cinema programmes, menus, cigarette cards, the lot. You will find it difficult to drag yourself away. ✆ *Calle del Almirante 23 • Map F3*

8 Plaisir Gourmet
This French-run labyrinthine paradise is for gourmets seeking top-quality Spanish olive oils, wines, herbs, spices, condiments and other goodies from around the world. ✆ *Calle Gravina 1 • Map R1*

9 Papelón
A unique and quirky gift shop, Papelón sells a collection of unusual items such as antique toys, kaleidoscopes, music boxes, sundials and zoetropes (cylindrical animation toys). ✆ *Calle Miguel Servet 9 • Map D6*

10 Alice in Wonderland
For some serious pampering, head to this wonderland of indulgence. This friendly, retro basement shop also offers manicures, pedicures and other beauty treatments. ✆ *Calle Tamayo y Baus 7 • Map F3*

Left **Ribeira do Miño** Right **Café Manuela**

🔟 Places to Eat and Drink

1 Arce
Chueca's top restaurant is not cheap, but it is a real gem. The menu changes regularly to make the most of seasonal produce, such as game and wild mushrooms. ◈ *Calle Augusto Figueroa 32 • Map Q1 • 91 522 0440 • Closed Sun D, Easter Sat & Sun • €€€€€*

2 Ribeira do Miño
This back-street Galician *marisquería* is well known for its good value shellfish, fresh fish and delicious *Crêpes Suzette*. ◈ *Calle Santa Brígida 1 • Map E3 • 91 521 9854 • Closed Mon, Aug • €€€€*

3 El Cisne Azul
Exquisite, large *tapas* are on the menu here. Try the wild mushrooms, rocket salad, lamb chops and steaks. ◈ *Calle Gravina 19 • Map R1 • 91 521 3799 • €€*

4 Café Oliver
Trendy bar-restaurant with modern interior. Serves Mediterranean cuisine and brunch on Sundays. ◈ *Calle del Amirante 12 • Map F3 • 91 521 7379 • €€€*

5 El Parnasillo
Cocktails are the speciality of this Malasaña bar *(see p64)*. ◈ *Calle de S Andrés 33 • Map D2 • 91 447 0079 • €€*

6 Pepe Botella
Relax at this old café with its red velvet banquettes and marble-topped tables. ◈ *Calle S Andrés 12 • Map D2 • 91 522 4309 • €€*

7 La Manduca de Azagra
This Navarre restaurant with its avant-garde decor is famed for its perfect vegetables, fresh fish and meats such as rack of lamb. *Tapas* are served at the bar. ◈ *Calle Sagasta 14 • Map E2 • 91 591 0112 • Closed Sun & public hols, Aug • €€€€*

8 La Bardemcilla
Owned by the sister of Spanish actor Javier Bardem, this lively café-restaurant serves typical Spanish dishes named after Bardem's films. ◈ *Calle de Augusto Figueroa 47 • Map Q1 • 91 521 4256 • €€€*

9 La Kitchen
This bright restaurant serves Spanish dishes with a modern twist. It is essential to book a table. ◈ *Calle Prim 5 • Map F3 • 91 360 4974 • Closed Sun & public hols • €€€€*

10 Café Manuela
More like a club for young people who drop in to chat, read the paper or play board games. Draught beer, cocktails and snacks. ◈ *Calle de S Vicente Ferrer 29 • Map D2 • 91 531 7037 • €*

Price Categories

For a three-course meal for one with half a bottle of wine (or equivalent meal), taxes and extra charges.

€	under €15
€€	€15–€25
€€€	€25–€35
€€€€	€35–€50
€€€€€	over €50

Above **Cervecería Santa Bárbara**

🔟 Tabernas

1 La Ardosa
This cosy *taberna* serves Guinness on tap, as well as excellent *tapas*. Try the *fabada* (bean and squid stew) *(see p64)*. ◈ Calle de Colón 13 • Map F3 • 91 521 4979 • €€

2 Cervecería Santa Bárbara
Large modern bar, popular with office workers, serving beer on tap. Good range of *tapas*. ◈ Plaza de S Bárbara 8 • Map E2 • 91 319 0449 • €€

3 Libertad 8
Relax at this Bohemian café-bar and listen to the singer-songwriters who perform in the back room. ◈ Calle Libertad 8 • Map F3 • 91 532 1150 • €€

4 El Bocaíto
Classic *tapas*. The prawn and garlic *tostadas* are wonderful *(see p66)*. ◈ Calle de la Libertad 6 • Map E3 • 91 532 1219 • Closed Sat L, Sun, Aug • €

5 El Comunista
One of the most authentic *tabernas* in the city, El Comunista offers simple home cooking. ◈ Calle de Augusto Figueroa 35 • Map E2 • 91 521 7012 • Closed Sun, Mon L • €€

6 Isla del Tesoro
One of the few vegetarian restaurants in the city offers international dishes. ◈ Calle Manuela Malasaña 3 • Map D2 • 91 593 1440 • Closed Sun L, 1 & 6 Jan, 25 Dec • €€

7 Bodegas el Maño
This old-fashioned wine cellar really looks the part, with fluted columns and painted barrels. Draught vermouth, beers and wines. A good range of *tapas* – the stuffed squid goes down a treat. ◈ Calle de la Palma 64 • Map D2 • 91 521 5057 • Closed Sun D • €

8 Café Isadora
Stylish bar decorated with posters of the legendary dancer Isadora Duncan. Jazz plays in the background while you chat over champagne cocktails and unusual liqueur coffees. ◈ Divino Pastor 14 • Map E3 • 91 445 7154 • Closed Mon • €

9 Café Comercial
Founded in 1887, and for that reason alone is a "must see". Tatty, *fin-de-siècle* decor. Internet café upstairs. ◈ Glorieta de Bilbao 7 • Map D2 • 91 521 5655 • €€

10 Taberna del Angel Sierra
Try the *escabeche de atún* (pickled tuna) at this *tapas* bar, which has Vermouth on tap. ◈ Calle Gravina 11 • Map R1 • 91 531 0126 • Closed Wed • €€

Note: Unless otherwise stated, all restaurants accept credit cards and serve vegetarian meals

Left **Chinchón** Right **Alcalá de Henares**

Comunidad de Madrid

THE COMUNIDAD DE MADRID *is a vast region covering 8,000 sq km (3,000 sq miles), with a population now exceeding five million. To the north of the capital is the Sierra de Guadarrama, a majestic mountain range, stretching more than 100 km (60 miles) east–west, and visitors to El Escorial, Valle de los Caídos, or Manzanares-el-Real will enjoy superb views as well as fresh mountain air. An excursion to the university town of Alcalá de Henares can easily be combined with Chinchón. Alternatively you could couple the latter with Aranjuez, an oasis of gardens and orchards in an otherwise parched landscape.*

Sights

1. El Escorial
2. Alcalá de Henares
3. Aranjuez
4. Chinchón
5. Manzanares-el-Real
6. Navacerrada
7. Nuevo Baztán
8. El Pardo
9. Pastrana
10. Valle de los Caídos

Cross, Valle de los Caídos

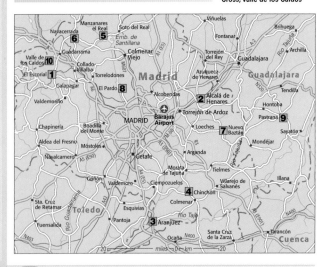

El Escorial

El Escorial
Apart from the famous monastery and the views of the Sierra, the attractions of El Escorial include the magnificent Coliseo, dating from 1771, and the two royal lodges *(see pp36–9)*.

Alcalá de Henares
This historic town has been designated a UNESCO World Heritage Site for its splendid Renaissance and Baroque architecture. It was the birthplace of Miguel de Cervantes, author of *Don Quixote*, and of the ill-fated Queen of England, Catherine of Aragon. The town's importance dates from the late 15th century when the head of the Spanish church, Cardinal Cisneros, founded a university here. A tour of the buildings, including the main hall with its *mudéjar* ceiling, is a must. Also worth seeing is Teatro Cervantes, the oldest public theatre in Europe, founded in the 17th century and restored in the 1990s. ◉ *Map B1 • Train from Atocha • University: Open for tours 10am–7pm Mon–Fri, 11am–7pm Sat, Sun & public hols • Adm*

Aranjuez
This gem of a town, awarded the status of UNESCO World Heritage Site in 2001, is a must see. The Palacio Real, summer residence of Spain's Bourbon rulers, is sumptuously decorated in the French style. No expense was spared either on the extravagant folly known as the Casa del Labrador, in the grounds near the River Tagus. The town has preserved some of its *corralas* – balconied wooden dwellings, built around a courtyard – and its bullring (Plaza de Toros). There are some excellent restaurants in the town and the Mercado de Abastos is a good source for picnic provisions. Aranjuez's strawberries, sold from roadside stalls, make the perfect dessert. The town is also famous for its asparagus. ◉ *Map B1 • Train from Atocha or themed Trena de la Fresa (Strawberry Train, see p53) • Palacio Real: Open for tours Apr–Sep: 10am–8pm; Oct–Mar: 10am–6pm (gardens open 8am–sunset) • Closed 1 Jan, 6 Jan, 1 May, 2 May, 30 May, 5 Sep, 24 Dec, 25 Dec, 31 Dec • Adm (except Wed for EU citizens)*

Chinchón
Life in this attractive little town revolves around the Plaza Mayor, the galleried main square, dating from the 16th century. Originally a cattle market, the square is the focus of a Holy Week procession on Good Friday, a passion play on Easter Saturday and bullfights in July and August. While you're here, try the local speciality, *anís*, a liquorice-flavoured liqueur (ask for "Chinchón"). Also worth seeing is the Iglesia de la Asunción, with a painting of the *Assumption of the Virgin* by Goya, whose brother was the local priest. ◉ *Map B1 • Bus La Veloz no. 337 from Plaza Conde Casal*

5 Manzanares-el-Real

This Sierra town is dominated by its well-preserved 15th-century castle. Almost as old is the church of Nuestra Señora de las Nieves (Our Lady of the Snows) with its 30-m (100-ft) high belltower. Hikers will enjoy the La Pedriza regional park with its massive granite boulders. ✎ *Map B1 • Bus no. 724 from Plaza de Castilla • Castle: Open Jun–Sep: 10am–5pm Tue–Fri, 10am–7pm Sat & Sun; Oct–May: 10am–5pm Tue–Sun • Closed Mon & public hols; Adm*

6 Navacerrada

At 1,860 m (6,100 ft) Navacerrada is the gateway to the Sierra de Guadarrama. Ski enthusiasts head straight for the Navacerrada Pass (Puerto de Navacerrada), but the town itself should not be overlooked. Apart from the parish church, which has an impressive 15th-century tower, and the 16th-century Church of the Nativity, the craft shops are worth a browse. Cafés abound on Plaza Mayor and there are hiking and cycling trails in the surrounding forests. ✎ *Map B1 • Bus 691 from Moncloa*

7 Nuevo Baztán

This settlement south of Alcalá de Henares was the brainchild of an 18th-century nobleman from Navarre, Juan de Goyeneche. Goyeneche built the estate so that he could supervise his various industrial enterprises, among the most advanced of the day. The Baroque palace, the domed church of St Francis Xavier and the workers' houses, designed by José de Churriguera, are the main attractions. ✎ *Map B1 • Road: A-2, then M-206 & M-219*

8 El Pardo

El Pardo is now a suburb of Madrid but was in open countryside when Enrico III built a hunting lodge here in the early 15th century. The Palacio del

Palacio del Pardo, El Pardo

Pardo was built by the Bourbons and substantially enlarged during the reign of Carlos III. More recently it was the official residence of General Franco. The tapestries, from sketches by Goya, are the outstanding feature. ◉ Map B1 • Bus No. 601 from Moncloa • Palacio del Pardo: Open daily Apr–Sep: 10am–8pm; Oct–Mar: 10am–6pm • Adm (free for EU citizens except Sat, Sun & public hols)

Pastrana

What draws visitors to the Alcarría region is the rugged scenery and peace and quiet. In Pastrana, first take a look at the Palacio Ducal in the main square. The Museo de la Colegiata (next to the church of the same name) has a splendid collection of 15th-century tapestries depicting the capture of Tangier by Alfonso V of Portugal. Just outside town is the Convento del Carmen, founded by St Teresa of Avila in the 16th century, with an exhibition on her life. ◉ Map B1 • Road A-2 to Guadalajara, then N-320 • Museo de Colegiata: Open daily 11:30am–2pm, 4:30–8pm (4:30–7pm winter); Adm • Convento del Carmen: Open 11am–2pm, 4–6:30pm (summer); 11am–1:30pm, 3–6:30pm (winter); Adm

Valle de los Caídos

The "Valley of the Fallen" was General Franco's memorial to his war dead from the Spanish Civil War (1936–9). The crypt and basílica, cut into the mountainside, were built by prison labourers. The most striking feature is a cross, 152 m (500 ft) high and 56 m (180 ft) wide. Franco himself is buried in the crypt. ◉ Map B1 • Road A-6 north, exit (salida) at M-600 • The valley is closed indefinitely to visitors • The Basílica still opens for worship between 10am and 5pm

A Day in Manzanares

Morning

⊙ To get to **Manzanares**, take bus No. 721 from Plaza de Castilla, alighting at Avenida de Madrid. There's a supermarket near the bus stop if you want to take a picnic. Take Calle del Castillo as far as Calle de Cañada and the restored 15th-century castle, from where there are good views of the storks fishing in the reservoir. Return along Calle de Cañada to the old town square, Plaza del Generalísimo, where you'll find several nice cafés and bars if you are ready for a coffee stop.

Cross the tree-sheltered Plaza del Raso, passing a small cemetery, and you'll come to the 16th-century Church of Our Lady of the Snows with its elegant Renaissance portico. Walk around the church for more views of the lake. Return to Plaza del Raso and take Calle Real, crossing the River Manzanares to the ruins of the old castle (castillo viejo). Then follow the river to the Chapel of the Holy Rock (Ermita de la Peña Sacra), built on a huge granite slab. Every Whitsun a procession in honour of the Virgin makes its way here from the cemetery.

Head to the Centric Plaza del Sagrado Corazón and stop for lunch at **Casa Goyo** (see p128).

Afternoon

Spend a leisurely afternoon enjoying the invigorating, fresh mountain air and splendid vistas of **La Pedriza** regional park.

Left **El Charolés** Right **Horizontal**

TOP 10 Historic Places to Eat

1 El Charolés
At what is considered to be the best restaurant in town, chef Manuel Miguez makes his renowned *cocido madrileño (see p62)* on Wednesdays. There is a summer terrace. ✆ *Calle de Floridablanca 24, San Lorenzo de El Escorial • Map A1 • 91 890 5975 • €€€€*

2 Las Viandas
This restaurant serves good, seasonal food. There is a small, summer terrace where you can enjoy a drink before your meal. ✆ *Plaza Constitución 2, San Lorenzo de El Escorial • Map A1 • 91 890 0986 • €€*

3 Fonda Genara
In an 18th-century building with theatre memorabilia, this reasonably priced restaurant has Castilian dishes, such as *rabo de toro* (bull's tail). Set-price menu. ✆ *Plaza S Lorenzo 2, El Escorial • Map A1 • 91 890 1636 • Closed Tue (summer) • €€€*

4 Horizontal
This classy restaurant has wonderful vistas of the sierra – book a terrace table in summer. It serves first-class international cuisine. ✆ *Camino Horizontal, El Escorial • Map A1 • 91 896 9199 • Closed Mon–Wed D in Winter • €€€*

5 Parrilla del Príncipe
Grilled fish is the speciality of this hotel-restaurant based in an 18th-century palace. ✆ *Calle Mariano Benebente 12, San Lorenzo de El Escorial • Map A1 • 91 890 1548 • Closed Tue, 15–28 Feb • €€*

6 Restaurant Botánico
Set within the imposing Hotel Botánico *(see p147)*, this is a great place to while away a summer's afternoon. It has a delightful shady terrace and serves a delicious *paella*. ✆ *Calle Timoteo Padros 16, San Lorenzo de El Escorial • Map A1 • 91 890 7879 • €€*

7 Croché Cafetin
Step back in time as you enter this Art Nouveau interior that boasts a handsome wooden bar counter, red velvet booths and aproned waiters. ✆ *Calle San Lorenzo 6, San Lorenzo de El Escorial • Map A1 • 91 890 5252 • €€*

8 La Parra
This traditional restaurant serves heart-warming country fare, such as stew made with beans and hare *(fabes con liebre)* and roast kid *(cabrito asado)*. ✆ *Calle Panaderos 15, Manzanares El Real • Map B1 • 91 853 9577 • Closed 21 Aug–12 Sep • €€*

9 El Rincón del Alba
Enjoy delectable fish and shellfish dishes here, with views of the Santillana marsh and La Pedriza mountain range. ✆ *Calle Paloma 2, Manzanares El Real • Map A1 • 91 853 9111 • €€€*

10 Casa Goyo
Situated in the village centre, this delightful restaurant serves traditional home cooking. ✆ *Plaza Sagrado Corazón 2, Manzanares El Real • Map A1 • 91 853 9484 • €€€*

Price Categories

For a three-course meal for one with half a bottle of wine (or equivalent meal), taxes and extra charges.

€	under €25
€€	€25–€35
€€€	€35–€55
€€€€	€55–€70
€€€€€	over €70

Above **Mesón Cuevas del Vino**

TOP 10 More Places to Eat

1 Terraza Jardín Felipe
This restaurant in a stone farmhouse is worth seeking out. Chef Felipe del Olmo is known for his stylish cooking – try the grilled hake in a delicious squid sauce. During the summer ask for a table on the large terrace. ◈ *Calle Mayo 2, Navacerrada • Map A1 • 91 853 1041 • €€*

2 Las Postas
This roadside hotel-restaurant serves Castilian meat dishes in an attractive dining room, the centrepiece of which is a 16th-century retablo. You can also enjoy live music here on Saturday nights. ◈ *Road M-601, 10.2 km, Navacerrada • Map A1 • 91 856 02 50 • €€€*

3 La Balconada
Nicely situated, "the balcony" overlooks Chinchón's main square. It serves typical Castilian fare such as *sopa de ajo* (garlic soup), *menestra* (lamb and vegetable stew) and *pepitoria de gallina* (chicken in an almond and egg sauce). ◈ *Plaza Mayor, Chinchón • Map B2 • 91 894 1303 • Closed Wed • €€€*

4 Mesón Cuevas del Vino
This old olive oil mill with its wine cellar offers traditional sierra cooking. Try the charcoal-grilled *chorizo* (spicy sausage), the beans, and almond dessert, before rounding off with the local liqueur, anís. ◈ *Calle de Benito Hortelano 13, Chinchón • Map B2 • 91 894 0206 • Closed Tue, Sun D • €€*

5 Mesón de la Virreina
Spanish and Mediterranean dishes. ◈ *Plaza Mayor 28, Chinchón • Map B2 • 91 894 0015 • €€€*

6 Casa José
The cuisine at this Michelin-star restaurant is based on home-grown produce. ◈ *Calle Abastos 32, Aranjuez • Map B2 • 91 891 1488 • Closed Sun D, Mon, Aug • €€€€*

7 Casa Pablo
This homely restaurant has the feel of an old tavern. Meat and fresh fish are the mainstays. ◈ *Calle Almíbar 42, Aranjuez • Map B2 • 91 891 1451 • Closed second week Jan, 1–15 Aug • €€€*

8 El Castillo 1806
Located in the grounds of Casa del Labrador, the house speciality here is *cordero al sarmiento* (grilled lamb). ◈ *Reales Jardines del Príncipe, Aranjuez • Map B2 • 91 891 3000 • Closed Mon • €€€*

9 Hostería del Estudiante
One of the dishes to try here is *migas castellanas* (bread-crumbs in garlic with fried eggs). It is part of the Parador Hotel. ◈ *Calle Colegios 8, Alcalá de Henares • Map B1 • 91 888 0330 • €€€*

10 Convento de San Francisco
Enjoy the local cuisine in the cloister of this 16th-century monastery in the centre of Pastrana. ◈ *Plaza del Deán, Pastrana • Map B2 • 94 937 0078 • €€€*

 Note: Unless otherwise stated, all restaurants accept credit cards and serve vegetarian meals.

STREETSMART

MADRID'S TOP 10

Left **Duty-free shop** Right **Summer in Madrid**

🔟 Planning Your Trip

1 Passports and Visas
No visa is required for citizens of EU countries, the USA, Canada, Australia, Iceland, Norway or Switzerland who are planning to stay for less than 90 days. Remember that passports need to be valid for three months beyond the end of your stay. Citizens of other countries should consult their Spanish embassy or consulate for information before travelling.

2 Choosing a Hotel
Generally in Madrid, you get what you pay for. In summer the essentials are air conditioning and double-glazed windows. The streets of the Old Town, tend to be very noisy throughout the night, so ask for a room at the back of the hotel. If space is important, ask about the size of the room; some can be very cramped. As Madrid has an excellent public transport system, it's worth considering a hotel away from the centre if you value peace and quiet. Also check whether the hotel offers reduced weekend rates.

3 Choosing a Restaurant
Madrid's best restaurants are in great demand, so it's important to book in advance of your trip. In any case it's a good idea to make a telephone booking 24 hours ahead, especially on Friday and Saturday evenings and for Sunday lunch.

4 What to See
Don't plan to see too much on a short stay, especially in summer when the afternoon heat makes sightseeing hard going. One of the great things about Madrid is its easy-going atmosphere – to get the most out of the city, do as the locals do and take long lunches and lots of coffee breaks.

5 When to Go
The best months to visit Madrid are May and September, when there's plenty of sunshine but the heat isn't too oppressive. Temperatures tend to be over 30° C (85° F) throughout July and August and the air doesn't cool down much until after midnight. November through March can be quite cold. Even then, however, the sun usually shines.

6 What to Pack
If you're visiting Madrid during winter, take warm jumpers, a raincoat and umbrella, as the weather can be unpredictable. In the summer remember to pack plenty of sun block, a head covering and sunglasses. *Madrileños'* dress code is smart but casual. Only the most formal restaurants require jacket and tie.

7 Electricity
The local power supply is 220 volts AC. Wall sockets have two-pin plugs. British shavers and hairdryers require an adaptor. If you're using an American appliance you'll need a transformer.

8 Currency
Travel with a small quantity of euro to pay for your first metro tickets or taxis. Cash dispensers (ATMs) are everywhere in Madrid and display symbols of which bank cards they accept. All major credit cards (Visa, MasterCard and American Express) are accepted.

9 Customs
For EU citizens there are no limits on goods that can be taken into or out of Spain, provided they are for your personal use. Outside the EU, you may import the following allowances duty-free: 200 cigarettes or equivalent in tobacco; 1 litre of spirits (exceeding 22 per cent) and 2 litres of wine; 50ml of perfume and 250ml of eau de toilette; gifts up to a value of €430.

10 Time Differences
Madrid is on Central European Time, 1 hour ahead of GMT, 6 hours ahead of Eastern Standard Time. Spanish summer time begins on the last Sunday in March and ends on the last Sunday in October.

 When planning your trip, note that most museums and galleries are closed on Mondays.

renfe

Left **RENFE railway sign** Right **Driving in Spain**

TOP 10 Getting to Madrid

1 Flights from Britain

British Airways and Iberia are the main carriers from London Heathrow, Manchester, London City and Glasgow; BA also flies from Birmingham. easyJet and Ryanair run regular flights from Liverpool, Luton, London Gatwick and Stansted, Bristol, Edinburgh and Manchester. Air Europa has some flights from London Gatwick. ✆ www.britishairways.com • www.iberia.com • www.easyjet.com • www.ryanair.com • www.air-europa.com

2 Flights from the USA

Iberia flies direct from New York, Miami and Chicago. Delta Air Lines also fly from the East Coast as does American Airlines. Air Europa offers less frequent but cheaper flights from New York. ✆ www.delta.com • www.air-europa.com • www.aa.com

3 Flights from Europe

All the major European airlines fly to Madrid, including KLM, Air France, Lufthansa and Alitalia.

4 Barajas International Airport

Madrid's airport is 12 km (10 miles) east of the city. There are four terminals: Terminals 1, 2 and 3 for Spanair, Air Europa, Ryanair, easyJet and other members of Star Alliance and Skyteam; Terminal 4 for Iberia flights and Oneworld Alliance flights. T4 is accessible via free shuttle buses that leave from the other terminals. If your departure gate is located in T4S, check-in at T4 and take the automatic train to the T4S building. Facilities include banks, hotel and rail reservation services, pharmacies, tourist information, left-luggage, post office, shops, places to eat and car hire. ✆ Barajas Airport: 91 393 6000

5 Getting into Madrid

Airport bus 200 runs regularly from T1 and T2 to the Avenida de America coach station. Taxis take at least 30 minutes. The Barajas metro link (line 8) from T2 and T4 takes 12 minutes to Nuevos Ministerios, and the Cercanías (overground) train runs from T4 to Madrid's main stations.

6 By Rail

You can travel direct from France or Portugal. The national Spanish rail operator is RENFE. Madrid's main stations are Estación de Chamartín in the north and Estación de Atocha in the south. Both are connected via the metro. Obtain tickets from stations, travel agents, or book over the telephone or Internet. ✆ RENFE: 902 32 03 20 • www.renfe.es

7 Chamartín Station

Chamartín serves trains from France, Catalonia and northern Spain. The AVE train serves Madrid–Segovia–Valladolid. Facilities include money exchange, cafés, car hire, post office, tourist information, hotel reservation, and shopping centre.

8 Atocha Station

Atocha (see p75) serves trains from southern Spain and Portugal. The AVE terminal handles the trains to Seville, Màlaga, Toledo, Barcelona, Valencia, Zaragoza, Huesca, Albacete, Cordoba and Cuenca. The station has exchange facilities and shops.

9 By Coach

The main coach station is Estación Sur de Autobuses. Travellers from France, Portugal and Spain's major cities arrive here. ✆ Estación Sur de Autobuses: corner Calle de Méndez Alvaro & Calle Retama • 91 468 4200

10 By Car

You need two days to drive from the UK, either via the cross-Channel ferry or the Channel tunnel. A third option is the ferry to Bilbao or Santander, followed by a four-hour drive from Bilbao or a five-hour drive from Santander. Road conditions are good, but expect heavy traffic on the outskirts of Madrid.

Left **Madrid bus** Right **Metro sign**

Getting Around Madrid

Tickets
1 A Metrobus ticket, valid for 10 journeys, is the most economical way of getting around the city and costs €9.30. You must stamp your ticket at the beginning of each journey. The Tourist Travel Pass is valid for up to 7 days and allows unlimited travel on all public transport. Tickets and travel passes are available from metro stations, *estancos* (tobacconists) and newspaper kiosks. Single metro tickets are sold in the station and cost €1.50.

Buses
2 Buses run from 6am until 11:30pm. Bus route maps can be obtained from tourist offices *(see p135)*. Night buses known as *buhos* (owls) depart from Plaza de Cibeles and run every 20 to 35 minutes. The price is the same as a day ticket and Metrobus tickets are valid.

Metro
3 Madrid's metro trains run every 3–5 minutes. Each of the 12 lines is colour-coded but you need to know the direction you're travelling in and the name of the end station. Services run from 6am to 1:30am. There is also the Metro Ligero (light railway) that serves the suburbs.

Taxis
4 City taxis are white with a diagonal red stripe and green light on the roof. They may be hailed or hired at a taxi rank. Check that the meter is not already running when you get in. There are extra charges for airport pick-up and travelling on Sundays, public holidays and at night. Motorbike taxis can be ordered from Moto City. § *Moto City: 91 000 1777*

Parking
5 Use one of the official underground car parks or park on the street in designated areas using the pay-and-display parking system – green lines indicate a limit of one hour, blue lines no more than two hours. Illegally parked cars may be impounded and should be recovered as soon as possible as the fines rise every hour.

Rental Cars
6 Anyone over the age of 21 can hire a car on presentation of a passport and valid driving licence (held for at least one year). You will also need an international insurance policy. All major companies are represented in Madrid and cars can be hired from the airport, main railway stations and large hotels.

Road Rules
7 Traffic drives on the right. Seat belts are compulsory for front-seat passengers. It's illegal to drive while wearing headphones or using a hand-held mobile phone. Drivers must carry two red hazard triangles, spare bulbs and a spare wheel. The speed limit on motorways is 110 kmph (65 mph), on main roads 90 kmph (55 mph), and 50 kmph (30 mph) within towns. Driving under the influence of alcohol or drugs is a serious offence incurring on-the-spot fines.

Tour Buses
8 The main tour bus company, Madrid Vision, offers several routes around the city. Buses depart daily from Gran Vía 32 and Sol. You can get on or off at any stop along the route. § *Madrid Vision: 91 779 1888 • www.madridvision.es*

Bikes and Scooters
9 Driving a motorcycle or moped is one way of avoiding traffic congestion and parking problems. Crash helmets must be worn, though many locals flout this law. Cycling in Madrid is generally dangerous. However, Bravobike offers tours that focus on quieter routes. § *Bravobike: www.bravobike.com*

Suburban Trains
10 The suburban train network, the *Cercanías*, is connected at various points to the metro. It is useful for reaching towns such as Alcalá de Henares and El Escorial *(see p125)*.

Left **Spanish newspapers** Right **Newspaper kiosk**

⑩ Sources of Information

1 Maps
An up-to-date map is an essential tool for getting around the city. One of the most detailed is *The Michelin A–Z* with a street index, available in bookshops and at newspaper kiosks. Easier to use but harder to read are the maps issued free by El Corte Inglés. The tourist offices and transport agencies have free bus and metro maps.

2 Municipal Tourist Information Office
The main city tourist office is in Plaza Mayor *(see pp18–19)*. It is well-stocked with maps, brochures and other information. The staff will help with accommodation but not book it for you.
◈ Plaza Mayor 27 • Map M5 • 91 588 1636 • Open 9:30am–8:30pm daily

3 Regional Tourist Office
This office covers the Greater Madrid area *(Comunidad de Madrid)* including the city itself. The staff are friendly and knowledgeable. ◈ Calle del Duque Medinaceli 2 • Map F5 • 902 100007 • Open 8am–3pm Mon–Sat, 9am–2pm Sun

4 Other Offices
Hi-tech tourist information mobile units situated at Palacio Real, Prado Museum and Caixa Forum are open during peak seasons and festivals. There are smaller tourist offices at Atocha and Chamartín railway stations, Plaza de Cibeles, Plaza del Callao and Plaza de Colón. Barajas airport *(see p133)* has two information centres in Terminals 2 and 4. Yellow information stands are also located in various terminals.

5 Walking Tours
From July to September the Plaza Mayor Tourist Office organizes a number of walking tours in English. Tours such as Essential Madrid cover the Royal Palace and major churches and monasteries, and also include versions for the disabled.

6 Listings Magazines
Free bilingual magazines can be found in tourist offices and tourist haunts such as Irish pubs, hotels and cafés. *InMadrid*, also published monthly in English, is an entertainment guide with listings on concerts and venues, as well as background articles on the Madrid cultural scene. It is available free from tourist offices, the Casa del Libro bookshop (Gran Vía 29), most Irish bars and some cafés in the centre. Those arriving by plane should look out for *Madrid Barajas*, which has tips and addresses, a map and background articles. It is bilingual, monthly and free.

7 Internet Sites
Two official sites are the City Tourist Office (www.esmadrid.com) and the Regional Tourist Office (www.descubre madrid.com). Both have good information in English and Spanish. Also try the official site for the whole of Spain (www.spain.info). Many major tourist attractions have their own sites.

8 Spanish Newspapers
If you can read Spanish, most daily papers such as *El País* and *El Mundo* have a supplement on Madrid including listings. *El País* also publishes an English-language supplement that rounds up Spanish news stories.

9 Foreign Newspapers
Foreign newspapers and some magazines such as *Time* are available on the day of publication from kiosks. The kiosk at the western end of Puerta del Sol is open 24 hours.

10 Spanish National Tourist Offices
Spain has tourist offices in most major cities abroad, including London (64 North Row, London, W1K 7DE, 020 7486 8034); Canada (2 Bloor St West, 34th floor, Toronto, Ontario M4W 3EZ, 416 961 3131) and the USA (60 East 42nd Street, Suite 5300, 53rd floor, NY 10165, 212 265 8822).

Left **Buskers** Right **Palacio Real**

TOP 10 Madrid on a Budget

1 Walking
Central Madrid is surprisingly compact and you can save money by walking between sights rather than taking the bus or metro. This is also a pleasant way to get to know the city.

2 Cheap Eats
If you're stopping for a coffee or snack, it's cheaper to stand at the bar than sit down. To save on lunch, order the *menú del día* or *plato combinado* – much cheaper than *à la carte*. *Tapas* is another way to eat cheaply *(see pp66–7)*. Some bars serve olives, crisps and nuts with drinks at no extra charge. Madrid is blessed with parks and green spaces, free to the public. Take a picnic to save buying a meal in a café or restaurant.

3 Buskers
While illegal, strictly speaking, busking is as common in Madrid as in other European cities and is a good source of free entertainment. Buskers perform in metro stations, in Retiro Park and on the street wherever they get the chance.

4 Free Museum Days
State museums, such as the Reina Sofía, are free on Saturday afternoons after 2:30pm, on weekday evenings and on Sundays. The Prado is free in the evenings and children

under 12 go free at Museo Thyssen-Bornemisza. National monuments managed by the *Patrimonio Nacional* (including the Palacio Real) are free for EU nationals on Wednesdays.

5 Concessions
Many museums and galleries offer free entry or reductions to the over 65s and students with an ISIC (International Student Identity Card). Under-18s can also gain reduced or free entry to museums, art galleries and other attractions. The Paseo del Arte combined ticket is the most economical way of visiting the three main art museums, although this does not include temporary exhibitions.

6 Cheap Accommodation
You can find acceptable accommodation in central Madrid for around €40 a night if you aren't too fussy about quality. There's only one camp site in Madrid itself, but many more in the Greater Madrid area. While facilities at the Madrid site are adequate, it's near the airport and noisy. The best youth hostel is Hostal Santa Cruz de Marcenado, a 5-minute walk from metro Argüelles. Book ahead. ◉ *Camping Osuna: Calle Jardines de Aranjuez 1; 91 741 0510 • Hostal Santa Cruz de Marcenado: Plaza Santa Cruz 6; 91 522 2441*

7 Breakfasts
While some hotels offer good-value breakfasts, many, especially at the cheaper end of the market, do not. You can save money by paying only for accommodation and taking breakfast in a local café, many of which offer reasonably priced English- or American-style breakfasts.

8 Madrid Card
This card gives you free entry to several museums as well as unlimited travel on the Madrid Visión tour bus and other discounts. 24-, 48- or 72-hour cards are sold at tourist offices, on Madrid Visión buses or over the internet. ◉ *www.madridcard.com*

9 Churches
While opening times are restricted, most churches are free to visit, or, in the case of cultural sites, cheap. They also hold free or inexpensive concerts, especially around Christmas, Holy Week *(Semana Santa)* and during the major summer and autumn cultural festivals *(see pp54–5)*.

10 Public Transport
Buy the economical Metrobus ticket, valid for 10 journeys, or the Tourist Travel Pass *(see p134)*. Keep track of the number of rides you've done, to avoid running out (ticket machines indicate how many journeys are left).

Left **Driving in Madrid** Right **Tourist queue**

TOP 10 Things to Avoid

1 Driving in Madrid
Traffic jams, problems with parking and risk-taking motorists make driving in central Madrid a frustrating and stressful experience, best avoided. On the other hand, hiring a car is a convenient way to explore the towns of Greater Madrid.

2 Crime
Madrid is a reasonably safe city providing you take the usual precautions like avoiding poorly lit backstreets after dark. Pickpockets are active on the metro and around Sol, Rastro and Lavapiés. Carry valuables in a belt pouch or similar, not in a pocket. Do not wear bags over one shoulder or leave them visible in restaurants. Never leave bags in your car, even the boot – your insurance won't provide cover. Thieves recognize the registration plates of hire cars and target them.

3 Taking Luggage on the Metro
You are not supposed to take large items of luggage on the metro, except to the airport on line 8. It may also help to be aware of the fact that not many metro stations have lifts, so taking big bags up and down the stairs can be difficult. Visitors on a budget may have no alternative, but it is best avoided, especially during rush hour.

4 Red Light District
Steer clear of the red light district, north of Gran Vía, even in the daytime, especially Calle de Valverde and Calle del Barco, and also Calle de la Montera to the south of Gran Vía. Single women should be particularly careful. If you do have to pass through, look as if you know where you're going and keep an eye on your valuables.

5 Parks at Night
Parks are safe during the daytime, but all should be avoided after dark. Especially dangerous at night is Casa de Campo, a notorious area for prostitution and drug dealing.

6 August and Public Holidays
The month of August is deadly quiet as most *Madrileños* take their annual summer holidays at this time. While most tourist sights remain open to the public, many bars and restaurants are closed. Also bear in mind that many shops are closed on public holidays.

7 Over-tipping
When eating out in restaurants and cafés, check your bill to see if a service charge has been included. If not, you should leave small change to the value of around 5 per cent of the bill. Taxi drivers will also expect a tip of around 5 per cent for longer journeys.

8 Queues
If you're planning on visiting the most popular sights, such as the Prado and the Palacio Real, arrive 15 or 20 minutes before the official opening time. The small inconvenience may well save you time in the long run as queues lengthen quickly. Arriving early is also the best way to avoid large, guide-led groups. Spanish queues at bus-stops and other places sometimes appear haphazard, but you will soon discover everyone knows his or her place.

9 Transport Fines
Remember to frank your metro or bus ticket in the machine as you start your journey and keep it handy in case an inspector asks to see it. Anyone without a validated ticket will have to pay an on-the-spot fine. Although you'll see many locals light up on metro escalators, it's illegal to smoke anywhere on the system and on buses. Again, offenders are subject to fines.

10 Beggars
Beggars are all too common a sight on the streets of Madrid, on the metro and outside churches. It's up to you whether you offer small change. The homeless have their own magazine – genuine sellers wear ID and will be carrying several copies.

Left **Madrid terrace café** Right **Confectioners**

TOP 10 Eating and Drinking Tips

Eating Patterns

Madrileños tend to eat frequently, but on a small scale. The main meal is lunch *(la comida)*, usually taken around 2pm, and restaurants are particularly busy at this time. Breakfast is a light affair, though reinforced with a mid-morning snack. Dinner is eaten around 10pm or later with another snack *(la merienda)* filling the gap.

Tapas

Originally a covering to keep the flies off a glass of wine, *tapas* (from the Spanish for "lid") is now a national institution. Relatively few of these snacks are free nowadays, although you may strike lucky. You may see the word *pincho* or *canapé* alternating with *tapas. Raciones* are double portions of the same, usually large enough for sharing.

Menú del Día

Most restaurants, cafés, even bars offer this set-price three-course option, usually at lunch. The price normally includes bread, wine or beer (or a non-alcoholic drink). Standards vary, but generally speaking you get what you pay for. The choice of first courses typically includes soup or *paella*, while the main meal consists of a fish or meat dish. Coffee is sometimes offered instead of dessert.

Combinados

If you're not feeling hungry enough for a full three-course lunch, the *plato combinado* will probably suffice. This is a one-course meal, with a little extra, for example a drink, salad or dessert.

Restaurantes and Tabernas

Nowadays the distinction between the two is largely artificial, though as a rule of thumb, a *taberna* will have a bar counter and will offer cheaper meals, served in a more informal atmosphere. While the word *taberna* suggests an inn or hostelry, more and more modern restaurants are usurping the term.

Cafés

Before the Civil War there were dozens of cafés around Sol and Gran Vía known as *tertulias* – unofficial discussion clubs where leisurely talk was more important than the drink. Very few have survived – exceptions include the Gijón *(see p79)* and the Comercial.

Pastelerías

Madrileños are notoriously sweet-toothed and cakes and pastries on sale here will certainly fill a hole if you don't have the time or appetite for a full sit-down meal. Some *pastelerías* also sell sandwiches, but only a few have seating areas.

Service

Waiter service is usually efficient until it comes to getting the bill. If you're in a hurry, either ask for the bill *(la cuenta)* with the last course or get the waiter's attention by calling *"perdone, la cuenta"* ("excuse me, the bill"). Value Added Tax (IVA) at 8 per cent is automatically added to bills, but not a service charge. A tip of up to 5 per cent is expected.

Bars

There are numerous words for bar – *bodega, cervecería, tasca, bar de copas* or just plain *bar*. Almost all serve food, usually *tapas* or other snacks. You pay a little more if you are served at table rather than drink at the counter. Bills are usually paid on leaving the bar, rather than after each round, though in late-night bars it's pay-as-you-buy. Even midweek it's possible to get a drink up to 1am in most places, and until 3am at weekends. *Madrileños* still on the town after that time often round off the evening with *chocolate con churros* – hot chocolate and doughnuts.

Street Markets

There are numerous markets in Madrid selling fruit, vegetables, meat, fish and bread. They're ideal for picnics and for soaking up the local atmosphere.

Left **VIPS chain store sign** Right **Madrid shopping street**

Shopping Tips

Opening Times
In general, shops in Madrid are open Monday to Saturday from 10am to 2pm and 5pm to 8:30pm. Most downtown shops are also open on Sundays and holidays. Opening hours for department stores and chains are Monday to Sunday 10am to 9pm.

Shopping Malls
Many high street brands and some of the top Spanish and international designers are represented in shopping malls, where you will also find cinemas, restaurants and large supermarkets. The most convenient for tourists are ABC Serrano and El Jardín de Serrano *(see p82)*.

Chains
There are a number of very useful chains in Madrid with extended opening hours. The most important is VIPS, which has branches all over the city. Most have cafeterias and sell a wide range of goods, including newspapers, drinks, batteries and other items *(see p93)*.

Tax-Free Shopping
Non-EU citizens can ask for a refund of Value Added Tax (IVA) on purchases in excess of €90.15. This can save you from 18 per cent of the cost price. You must ask for a cashback form at the time of purchase.

Crafts
Traditional Spanish fans are not only the preserve of flamenco dancers; they are still used by many women to ward off the heat in summer and are not expensive. Embroidered shawls and lace *mantillas* are sold in specialist outlets like Casa Jiménez *(see p48)*. Leather goods aren't necessarily cheaper than back home, but are of exceptional quality; try Loewe *(see p83)*. The arcades of Plaza Mayor are a good starting point for ceramics and other souvenirs *(see pp18–19)*.

Food and Drink
Spain's number one gastronomic export is not wine, surprisingly, but *jamón* (ham). There are numerous varieties to choose from – carry out your own tasting survey in the city's *tapas* bars before homing-in on your favourite. Wine shopping has become easier with the arrival of wine supermarkets, many of which have cut-price offers.

Antiques
Look for high-quality antiques in the Salamanca district, especially on Calle de Jorge Juán, Calle de Claudio Coello and the mall on Calle de Lagasca (Centro de Anticuarios Lagasca). The galleries on Ribera de Curtidores *(see p22)* are also worth checking out,

as is Calle de Prado, near Sol. For the lower end of the market, head for the Rastro *(see pp22–3)*.

Fashion and Clothes
The hunting ground for fashion victims is the Salamanca district which showcases Spanish and international designers. A good starting point is Calle de Serrano *(see p80)* or Calle Ortega y Gasset. There are more haute couture stores in Chueca (Calle del Almirante and Calle del Conde de Xiquena). For mainstream clothes, the best areas are Calle de Fuencarral and the streets around Sol.

Clothes Sizes
Clothing and shoe sizes differ from those of the UK and the US. Women's size 12 (10 in the US), for example is size 40 in Spain. Men's shirt collar size 15, is 38 in Spain. Shoe size 5 (7 in the US) is 38 in Europe, size 10 (11 in US) is 43. Most main stores have conversion charts and knowledgeable staff can also provide advice.

Sales
Stores sell off surplus stock at bargain prices during the sales. These take place twice a year – in January and February and July to August. Also look out for seasonal reductions *(rebajas de temporada)*.

Left **Bank** Right **Spanish telephone sign**

Banking and Communications

1 Currency
In January 2002 Spain joined 11 other European countries in converting its currency to the euro. The peseta ceased to be legal tender at the end of February 2002, after a stint of more than 140 years as the national currency. The euro is subdivided into 100 céntimos. Euro banknotes have the following denominations: 5, 10, 20, 50, 100, 200 and 500. Euro coins come in eight denominations: €1, €2, and 1, 2, 5, 10, 20 and 50 céntimos. Visitors from outside the eurozone should check the exchange rates at the time of travel.

2 Changing Money and Bank Hours
Bureaux de change are found throughout the city, especially around Puerta del Sol (see p87). There are also 24-hour counters at Barajas airport (see p133), the two mainline stations, El Corte Inglés (see p88) and other central department stores and major hotels. Many banks also have a currency exchange desk and will accept travellers' cheques as well as cash. Banking hours are Monday to Friday, 8:30am to 2pm. Some branches also open, September to June only, on Saturdays from 9am to 1pm. During the San Isidro festival (see p54) all banks close at midday.

3 Cash Dispensers
ATMs abound in Madrid and are the easiest way of getting hold of cash. Those accepting internationally recognized cards will give you a choice of several languages, including English.

4 Credit Cards
Spain is more of a cash society than some other European countries. In Madrid, most hotels and restaurants will take credit cards, but some *pensions*, *tabernas* and *tapas* bars will only accept cash. Shops take cards but may ask to see some identification.

5 Post
The Main Post Office (Palacio de Communicaciones) in Plaza de Cibeles is a tourist sight in its own right (see p73). Opening hours are Monday to Friday 8:30am to 9pm, Saturday 8:30am to 2pm. For other post offices (correos), look for the yellow sign and the crown and post-horn logo. These open Monday to Friday 8:30am to 2:30pm, Saturday 9am to 1pm. Postboxes are yellow.

6 Estancos
Another useful place to buy stamps is a tobacconist (estanco) as queues are shorter than in post offices. These small shops also sell metrobus tickets and are designated with a brown-and-yellow sign.

7 Telephones
All Madrid phone numbers are prefixed with 91, followed by seven digits. To phone Spain from overseas, dial the code 00 34. Some public telephones take coins, others accept phonecards which are on sale at post offices, tobacconists and newspaper kiosks. Only a few take credit cards. Local calls are inexpensive and all calls are cheaper between 8pm and 8am, and at weekends and public holidays.

8 Internet
Most hotels, and café and restaurant chains in Madrid, such as Starbucks, provide their customers with free Internet access. Just ask the staff for the code to access the Wi-Fi.

9 Newspapers and Magazines
A wide range of foreign daily journals can be found at the newspaper kiosks that are sited around Plaza de Cibeles and Puerta de Sol.

10 Television
Most big hotels subscribe to satellite and cable TV. If you're staying in lower priced accommodation you may only have access to the seven free Spanish channels – TVE1, TVE2, Antena 3, Telecinco, Cuatro, Telemadrid and La Sexta.

Left **Spanish policeman** Centre **Fire engine** Right **Pharmacy sign**

🔟 Security and Health

1 Police
Police stations are listed in the *Yellow Pages (Páginas Amarillas)*. You should report all crimes including theft and lost property for insurance purposes. The Foreign Tourist Assistance Service (SATE) offers multilingual assistance 24 hours a day. You can call them on 90 210 2112. If you lose your passport, inform your embassy or consulate and the police. ◈ *Central Police Station: Calle Leganitos 19, 91 548 8537*

2 Hospitals
There are casualty departments *(Urgencias)* at Hospital General Gregorio Marañón and Hospital La Paz. Other Spanish hospitals are listed in the *Yellow Pages* by area. For English-speaking doctors and dentists contact the Anglo-American Medical Unit. ◈ *Hospital General Gregorio Marañón: Calle Dr Esquerdo 46, 91 586 8000 • Hospital La Paz: Paseo de la Castellana 261, 91 727 7000 • Anglo-American Medical Unit, Calle Conde de Aranda 1, 91 435 1823*

3 Ambulances
If you need an ambulance urgently, dial the city service (SAMUR) on 092 or 112, Red Cross Ambulances *(ambulancias de la Cruz Roja)* or the emergency number. ◈ *Red Cross Ambulances: 91 522 2222*

4 Pharmacies
An illuminated green cross indicates a pharmacy *(farmacia)* which is usually open 10am to 2pm, 5pm to 8pm Monday to Saturday. If closed, the address of the nearest alternative will be displayed in the window. Pharmacists will treat minor ailments as well as give medical advice – most speak a little English – but bring any prescription medicines with you as you may not be able to find the exact equivalent. Pharmacists also have information about health centres and doctors.

5 Dentists
Ask at your hotel for the nearest dentist or consult the *Yellow Pages*. Clínica de Prado covers 24-hour emergencies. Expect to pay as dentistry is not covered by the EHIC card. ◈ *Clínica de Prado: Calle Luchana 6, Floor 4, 91 188 9472*

6 Mugging
Mugging is not very common in Madrid, but it does happen. Avoid travelling alone at night on dark, empty streets, travelling in empty metro carriages and carrying large amounts of cash.

7 Pickpockets
As in most cities, pickpockets operate in crowds and especially at tourist sights. Keep wallets close to hand and be as inconspicuous as possible when handling money in the street.

8 Crossing the Road
Madrileños are not the most careful of drivers and tend to take risks – jumping red lights is commonplace. Pedestrians do not automatically have right of way on crossings, and an orange flashing light is generally regarded as "go" by drivers. Crossings are often located at street corners, so keep an eye on cars turning from side roads.

9 Women Travellers
Generally, Spanish men are courteous but chauvinistic. Throw-away compliments *(piropos)*, sometimes accompanied by a hissing sound to gain attention, are common. A firm rebuttal usually discourages unwelcome advances.

10 Insurance
EU citizens can avoid medical charges by carrying a valid European Health Insurance Card (EHIC), which must be obtained before travelling. Other nationals must take out private medical cover.

Emergency Nos.
Police: 091
Medical Advice: 061
Municipal Police: 092
Tourist Assistance: 902 102 112
Emergencies: 112
Fire: 112

Left **Ritz** Right **Westin Palace**

TOP 10 Luxury Hotels

1 Santo Mauro
Small, elegant hotel enjoying a secluded leafy location, yet only five minutes' walk from the Paseo de la Castellana. The former palace was refurbished in the 1990s in a mixture of classical and modern styles; the ballrooms now serve as conference rooms while the library is a gourmet restaurant with terrace. Indoor swimming pool. ◈ *Calle Zurbano 36 • Map F1 • 91 319 6900 • www. marriott.com • €€€€€*

2 Ritz
Madrid's oldest luxury hotel remains true to the traditional values of refined comfort and impeccable service. The *belle époque* decor and furnishings extend to all 167 rooms, but are seen to best effect in the restaurant, overlooking a flower-filled garden. Facilities include a solarium, gym and sauna. ◈ *Plaza de la Lealtad 5 • Map F4 • 91 701 6767 • www.ritz. es • Dis. access • €€€€€*

3 Westin Palace
This hotel opened in 1913 and has been wowing guests ever since with its opulence. The palatial facilities include 18 banqueting and conference rooms, a business centre, fitness suite and gourmet restaurant. ◈ *Plaza de las Cortes 7 • Map E4 • 91 360 8000 • www.westinpalacemadrid. com • Dis. access • €€€€€*

4 Miguel Angel
From the outside, this modern hotel overlooking Paseo de la Castellana conforms with the high-rise architecture typical of the business district, but the interior, refurbished with antiques, is a surprise. Facilities include conference and banqueting suites, sun terrace, indoor swimming pool, sauna, gym and disco. The hotel's M29 restaurant serves innovative Mediterranean cuisine. ◈ *Miguel Angel 29–31 • Map F1 • 91 442 0022 • www.occidental hotels.com • €€€€*

5 Orfila
Built in 1886 as a palatial townhouse, the Orfila is located in a leafy part of town near Colón. The 20 rooms and 12 suites are tastefully decorated in soft pinks and yellows to create a relaxed ambience. A small restaurant overlooks a secluded garden. ◈ *Orfila 6 • Map F2 • 91 702 7770 • www. hotelorfila.com • €€€€€*

6 Villa Magna
What attracts celebrities like Madonna to this hotel is the service and attention to detail. The restaurant has made it a by-word for dining. The 150 rooms are spacious and elegant. ◈ *Paseo de la Castellana 22 • Map G2 • 91 587 1234 • www. villamagna.com • Dis. access • €€€€€*

7 Villa Real
The elegant Villa Real opened in 1989. The antique decor extends to the luxury suites, while the foyer is decorated with Roman mosaics. Facilities run to a fitness suite, conference centre and gourmet restaurant. ◈ *Plaza de las Cortes 10 • Map E4 • 91 420 3767 • www.derbyhotels.es • Dis. access • €€€€*

8 Husa Serrano Royal
This small hotel is close to the designer stores of Calle Serrano (see p82). The rooms are large and comfortable. Facilities include a garage and business centre. ◈ *Calle de Marqués de Villamejor 8 • Map G1 • 91 576 9626 • www.husa.es • €€€*

9 Wellington
During the San Isidro festival in May, this hotel is the first choice of Spain's top bullfighters. Its Michelin-starred restaurant serves Japanese–Spanish fusion cuisine. The swimming pool is another plus. ◈ *Calle Velázquez 8 • Map G3 • 91 575 4400 • www.hotel-wellington.com • €€€€€*

10 Gran Meliá Fenix
This gorgeous hotel is located near Plaza Colón. It is handy for the sights and the Salamanca shopping district. ◈ *Calle Hermosilla 2 • Map G2 • 91 431 6700 • www.solmelia. com • Dis. access • €€€€€*

Note: *Unless otherwise stated, all hotels accept credit cards, have en-suite bathrooms and air conditioning*

Price Categories

For a standard, double room per night (with breakfast if included), taxes and extra charges.

€ under €70
€€ €70–€120
€€€ €120–€180
€€€€ €180–€240
€€€€€ over €240

Above **NH Lagasca**

TOP10 Comfortable Hotels

1 Trafalgar
Located in a residential neighbourhood north of the centre, this 3-star hotel will suit visitors who like peace and quiet. Rooms are clean and modern and equipped with satellite TV. The hotel has its own bar, restaurant and conference room. ⊗ Calle Trafalgar 35 • Map E1 • 91 445 6200 • www.bestwesternhoteltrafalgar.com • €€€

2 NH Lagasca
Shopaholics need look no further than this good value, 3-star hotel, close to the boutiques of Calle Serrano. Built in the early 1990s, all rooms have well-designed bathrooms. The hotel also offers an airport shuttle service. ⊗ Calle de Lagasca 64 • Map G3 • 91 575 4606 • www.nh-hotels.com • €€€

3 Conde Duque
A medium-sized hotel in a quiet, residential neighbourhood, with good transport links to the centre. Rooms are comfortable and tasteful and are equipped with satellite TV. ⊗ Plaza Conde del Valle Súchil 5 • Map C2 • 91 447 7000 • www.hotelcondeduque.es • Dis. access • €€€

4 Tryp Ambassador
The former palace of the Dukes of Granada de Ega, this hotel has an excellent location near the Opera House and only a few minutes' walk from the Palacio Real and Gran Vía. The courtyard has been converted into a glass-roofed atrium and bar. Rooms are tastefully decorated and equipped with satellite TV. ⊗ Cuesta de Santo Domingo 5 • Map L3 • 91 541 6700 • www.tryphotels.com • €€€

5 Emperatriz
This modern 4-star hotel is situated on the fringes of Salamanca, so it's no surprise that many of its regular clients are from the fashion and media worlds. All rooms have similar wooden furnishings but only some have a terrace. The restaurant serves Spanish and international cuisine. ⊗ Calle Lopez de Hoyos 4 • Metro Ruben Darío• 91 563 8088 • www.hotel-emperatriz.com • €€€€

6 Silken Puerta de América
Designed by French architect Jean Nouvel, this modern hotel is located on one of the main arteries into the centre of Madrid. Each of its 12 floors has been designed by a well-known architect or designer including Sir Norman Foster, Arata Isozski, Zaha Hadid and Javier Mariscal. The hotel boasts a good restaurant. ⊗ Avenida de América 41 • 91 744 5400 • www.hotelpuertamerica.com • €€€€€

7 Velázquez
The main advantage of this 4-star hotel is the size of the rooms – half include a lounge. The facilities include an on-site restaurant and six meeting rooms. ⊗ Calle Velázquez 62 • Map G3 • 91 575 2800 • www.hotelvelazquez.com • €€€

8 BW Arosa
Just off the Gran Vía, the Arosa has 126 sound-proofed rooms including 16 zen rooms. There is also a Japanese restaurant. ⊗ Calle de la Salud 21 • Map N3 • 91 532 1600 • www.hotelarosa.es • €€€

9 Aparthotel Eraso
These 31 apartments, each comprising twin bedroom, bathroom, kitchenette and garage, are located near the bullring at Las Ventas. There's easy access to Barajas airport and the IFEMA exhibition centre. Facilities include cleaning twice a week, a business centre and TV. ⊗ Calle de Ardemans 13 • 91 355 3200 • Metro Diego de León • www.hotelesquo.com • €€

10 Monte Real
In the exclusive Puerto Hierro district, northwest of the city yet only a 15-minute cab ride away. Facilities include tennis courts, sauna, pool and a golf course nearby. ⊗ Arroyofresno 17 • 91 736 5273 • www.hotelmontereal.com • €€€

Left **Inglés** Right **NH Nacional**

🔟 Hotels Handy for the Sights

Inglés
Founded in 1886, this family-run hotel is close to the Prado and the night-life around Sol and Plaza Santa Ana. The rooms are spotless and comfortable, though those overlooking the street can be noisy; nevertheless, the location makes Inglés excellent value. It is best to book ahead, as the hotel is popular. ॐ *Calle Echegaray 8 • Map Q5 • 91 429 6551 • www.hotelinglesmadrid. com • No air con • €€€*

Liabeny
Close to Sol, Gran Vía and the shops of Calle Preciados, this modern 4-star hotel has been done up with wooden and leather furnishings throughout. The rooms are on the small side, but clean and comfortable. Service is attentive and there's a certain old-world charm about the place. ॐ *Calle Salud 3 • Map N3 • 91 531 9000 • www.liabeny.com • €€€*

Urban
Combining luxury with contemporary design, Urban is well located between Puerta del Sol and Paseo del Prado, near the city's main museums. The sophisticated decor extends throughout the restaurant and "Glass Bar", both of which are highly recommended. ॐ *Carrera de San Jerónimo 34 • Map R4 • 91 787 7770 • www.derbyhotels.com • €€€€€*

NH Alcalá
This 4-star hotel is handy for the Retiro, the art museums and the fashion boutiques of Salamanca. The building is modern but the ambience is old-world. All rooms were refurbished in the 1990s; try for one overlooking the leafy courtyard. ॐ *Calle de Alcalá 66 • Map G3 • 91 435 1060 • www.nh-hotels. es • €€€*

NH Nacional
A large 4-star hotel in an imposing early 20th-century building opposite Atocha railway station. The location is perfect for the "golden triangle" of art museums. The hotel has its own bar and restaurant and the stylish rooms are equipped with satellite TV (some have balconies). ॐ *Paseo del Prado 48 • Map F5 • 91 429 6629 • www.nh-hotels. es • Dis. access • €€€*

Santo Domingo
This modernized hotel, convenient for the Palacio Real and the Gran Vía, is furnished with strategically placed statues and old paintings to give it a touch of ele-gance. Though small, the rooms are comfortable – try for one on the fifth floor where there are tiny balconies with views of the city. ॐ *Calle San Bernado 1 • Map L2 • 91 547 9800 • www.accor hotels.com • Dis. access • €€€€*

NH Embajada
Located in the chic district of Chamberí, this hotel includes a restaurant and meeting rooms, while the pleasant rooms have TV and hair-dryers. A special breakfast is available for early risers. ॐ *Calle Sta Engracia 5 • Map D2 • 91 594 0213 • www. nh-hotels.com • €€€*

Cortezo
This 92-room hotel is excellent value, given its location near the Rastro and Plaza Mayor, and its spotless rooms are furnished with antiques. There's a cafeteria and an airport shuttle on request. ॐ *Calle Doctor Cortezo 3 • Map N5 • 91 369 0101 • www.mercure.com • Dis. access • €€*

Mercure Plaza España
This 4-star hotel is in a quiet residential street near the leafy surround-ings of Parque del Oeste. The rooms with a balcony are the most attractive. The piano bar is a good place to relax. ॐ *Calle Tutor 1 • Map B2 • 91 541 9880 • www.accorhotels. com • Dis. access • €€€€*

Moderno
A 3-star option on one of Madrid's most historic streets. Rooms (some with balcony) are restful, with double glazing. Breakfast is not included. ॐ *Calle del Arenal 2 • Map M4 • 91 531 0900 • www. hotel-moderno.com • €€€*

Note: Unless otherwise stated, all hotels accept credit cards, have en-suite bathrooms and air conditioning

Streetsmart

Price Categories

For a standard, double room per night (with breakfast if included), taxes and extra charges.

€ under €70
€€ €70–€120
€€€ €120–€180
€€€€ €180–€240
€€€€€ over €240

Above **Aristos**

🔟 Business Hotels

1 Eurobuilding
This high-rise north of the city was designed with business customers in mind. The facilities include 20 conference rooms, a business centre and interpreting services, while each bedroom has Internet and fax. The Palace of Congresses is only a short walk away and the IFEMA Exhibition Centre and Barajas airport are 15 minutes' drive away. Clients can relax on the terraces, by the pool or in the gym and sauna. ⓢ *Calle Padre Damián 23 • 91 353 7300 • www.nh-hotels.es • Dis. access • €€€€*

2 Aristos
The main advantage of this small, modern hotel is the location – 15 minutes' drive from the airport, IFEMA Exhibition Centre, Palace of Congresses and the city. All rooms have bathrooms with hydromassage showers. The restaurant serves Mediterranean cuisine and has a small terrace. ⓢ *Avenida de Pío XII 34 • 91 345 0450 • www.hotelaristos.com • €€€*

3 Orense
This 4-star hotel has an excellent location in Madrid's business district. Facilities include three meeting rooms, a private dining room and Wi-Fi Internet service. ⓢ *Calle de Pedro Teixeira 5 • 91 597 15 68 • www.rafaelhoteles.com • €€€€*

4 AC-Aitana
Fully renovated for business clients, the facilities of this functional but quiet 4-star hotel include on-site parking, restaurant and bar, reading room, fitness centre and two small conference rooms. All rooms are equipped with satellite TV, two phones and Wi-Fi Internet service. ⓢ *Paseo de la Castellana 152 • Map F3 • 91 458 4970 • www.marriott.com • Dis. access • €€€€*

5 Meliá Barajas
On the approach road to Barajas airport, this 229-room modern hotel is convenient for the IFEMA Exhibition Centre. Rooms are comfortable and the hotel facilities include a garden, outdoor pool, restaurants, gym, and meeting rooms. ⓢ *Avenida de Logroño 305 • 91 747 7700 • www.solmelia.es • Dis. access • €€€*

6 Rafael Atocha
For those not travelling on an expense account, this modern 3-star hotel offers exceptional value. Near Atocha railway station, all 245 rooms have satellite and cable TV, and marble bathrooms with direct-dial phone. Facilities include a business centre, restaurant and garage. ⓢ *Calle Méndez Alvaro 30 • Map F6 • 91 468 8100 • www.rafaelhoteles.com • Dis. access • €€€*

7 Catalonia Gran Vía
Conveniently situated for the stock exchange, this comfortable hotel is also handy for the sights. Modern rooms with satellite TV. Facilities include a Catalan restaurant, gym, sauna and Jacuzzi. ⓢ *Gran Vía 9 • Map R3 • 91 531 2222 • www.hoteles-catalonia.es • €€€*

8 Husa Moncloa
Good for business travellers on a budget and just five minutes' walk from Plaza de España. Hotel facilities include a conference room, bar and restaurant. ⓢ *Calle Serrano Jover 1 • Map B2 • 91 542 4582 • www.hotelhusamoncloa.com • Dis. access • €€€*

9 Confortel Madrid Suites
Located north of the centre, this hotel has 120 suites, all equipped with satellite TV. Facilities include a restaurant offering international cuisine. ⓢ *Calle López de Hoyos 143 • Metro Alfonso XIII • 91 744 5000 • www.confortelhoteles.com • Dis. access • €€€*

10 Meliá Avenida de América
Near the IFEMA exhibition centre and Barajas airport. Facilities include convention centre, swimming pool, gym and sauna. ⓢ *Calle Luca de Tena 36 • 91 423 2400 • http://es.solmelia.com • Dis. access • €€*

Recommend your favourite hotel on traveldk.com

Left **Mora** Right **Santander**

Budget Accommodation

Hostal Greco
This was once a brothel catering for a wealthy clientele that included members of Spain's aristocracy. Signs of its history include frescoes depicting women striking seductive poses. The location near the Gran Vía is excellent. ◎ *Calle Infantas 3, 2nd floor • Map R2 • 91 522 4632 • www.hostalgreco.com • Dis. access • €*

Hotel Asturias
This large early 20th-century building is considered a bargain on account of its location. All 170 rooms are clean, comfortable and in great demand, so it is necessary to book well in advance. ◎ *Calle de Sevilla 2 • Map Q4 • 91 429 6676 • www.hotel-asturias.com • No air con • €€*

Mora
Art lovers on a budget should look no further than this modest-sized hotel, just across the road from the Prado. Some rooms have views of the famous avenue. Room safes and satellite TV are other pluses. Popular, so book ahead. ◎ *Paseo del Prado 32 • Map F5 • 91 420 1569 • www.hotelmora.com • €€*

Hostal Carrera
An easy-going, friendly place with a great location near Sol and the nightlife of Santa Ana. The rooms are generously sized, but those over-looking the street can be noisy. ◎ *Carrera de San Jerónimo 30, 3rd floor • Map Q4 • 91 429 6808 • www.hostalcarrera.com • €*

Hostal Plaza d'Ort
In the heart of Madrid, this friendly hostel is convenient for the nightlife of Huertas and the art galleries on the Paseo del Prado. The 24 rooms are clean and nicely decorated and have TV and phone. There's also a bar and laundry service. ◎ *Plaza del Angel 13, 1st floor • Map P5 • 91 429 9041 • www.plazadort.com • €*

Santander
This rather quaint hotel, is conveniently located near the Prado. The high-ceilinged rooms are spotless, but those facing the street are noisy in summer. On the plus side, rooms are larger than usual and the English-speaking staff are very helpful. There is no breakfast or lunch service. ◎ *Calle Echegaray 1 • Map Q5 • 91 429 9551 • www.hotelsantander madrid.com • €€*

Hostal Gonzalo
A pleasant hostel in an historic part of Madrid, close to the museums of the Paseo del Prado. Some of the rooms have balconies with rooftop views of the city and are surprisingly quiet, bearing in mind that this area is also known for its nightlife. ◎ *Calle Cervantes 34, 3rd floor • Map F5 • 91 429 2714 • www.hostalgonzalo.com • €*

Hotel Francisco
This cosy little hotel is situated in the heart of Madrid and is only a stone's throw from Puerta del Sol, Plaza Mayor and the Palacio Real. It includes all the standard hotel amenities as well as a games room. ◎ *Calle Arenal 15 • Map D4 • 91 548 0204 • €*

Casón del Tormes
The location of this 3-star hotel, often used by tour companies, is excellent – just a few metres from the Gran Vía and with easy access to the Palácio Real. All rooms have direct-dial phone and satellite TV. A baby-sitting service is also available. ◎ *Calle del Río 7 • Map K1 • 91 541 9746 • www.hotelcasondeltormes.com • €€*

Hostal Persal
Overlooking a quiet square, yet surrounded by shops, bars and monuments, this hostel is excellent value. The comfortable rooms all have satellite TV and some overlook the courtyard. Also has its own coffee shop; a good place to get to know fellow guests and trade information. ◎ *Plaza del Angel 12 • Map P5 • 91 369 4643 • www.hostalpersal.com • €*

Above **ME Madrid**

Price Categories

For a standard, double room per night (with breakfast if included), taxes and extra charges.

€ under €70
€€ €70–€120
€€€ €120–€180
€€€€ €180–€240
€€€€€ over €240

Hotels with a Difference

Posada del Peine
This charming hotel, founded in 1610, is the oldest in Spain and is conveniently located on a pedestrian street in the heart of Old Madrid, close to the Plaza Mayor. Although some rooms are small, the decor is modern and there are computers and Wi-Fi in each room. Pets under 12 kg (26 lb) are allowed. ✪ Calle Postas 17 • Map M4 • 91 523 8154 • www.hotel-posadadelpeine.com • Dis. access • €€€

Ópera
As its name suggests, this comfortable 4-star hotel is close to the opera house. All rooms have satellite TV and some have balconies. The English-speaking staff are helpful. The waiters in the restaurant serenade guests with arias. ✪ Cuesta de S Domingo 2 • Map L3 • 91 541 2800 • www.hotelopera.com • €€

ME Madrid
Refurbishments have converted this beautiful early 1900s building into a modern hotel with excellent facilities and a trendy, penthouse bar. The hotel is a much-loved landmark, conveniently located close to Puerta del Sol (see p87) and the city's museums. ✪ Plaza de Sta Ana 14 • Map P5 • 90 214 4440 • www.memadrid.com • Dis. access • €€€€€

La Quinta de los Cedros
Located in a residential area close to the airport, this Renaissance-style mansion has been converted into a 4-star hotel. Bungalows with terraces overlooking a magnificent garden of cedars (from which the hotel takes its name) are also available. ✪ Calle Allendesalazar 4 • 91 515 2200 • www.quintade loscedros.com • €€€

Alicia Room-Mate
This modern hotel, conveniently located in the Plaza de Santa Ana, is a good choice for those keen to enjoy Madrid's nightlife. The colourful rooms have big windows that look out over this vibrant square. ✪ Calle del Prado 2 • Map Q5 • 91 389 6095 • www.room-matehotels.com • €€€

Sanvy
This 4-star hotel offers a large swimming pool, nightclub, hairdresser and excellent restaurant. The location is equally convenient. ✪ Calle Goya 3 • Map G2 • 91 576 0800 • www.nh-hotels.com • €€€

El Antiguo Convento
The convent was founded in 1670 by a Spanish nobleman and restored as a hotel by the distinguished Spanish architect José Ramon Duralde in 2001. The 17 rooms are tastefully decorated with antiques and overlook the cloisters, refectory and gardens. ✪ Calle de las Monjas, Boadilla del Monte • Bus 571, 573 • 91 632 2220 • www.elconvento.net • €€€€

NH Abascal
This hotel was once the Lebanese embassy. The decor is suitably aristocratic, with plenty of marble and wrought iron. The rooms are tastefully furnished (all are equipped with cable TV), and facilities include a sauna, gym and terrace restaurant. ✪ Calle José Abascal 47 • Map G2 • 91 441 0015 • www.nh-hotels.com • Dis. access • €€€€

Emperador
A great location overlooking Plaza de España. Its luxurious rooms (suites have Jacuzzi and hydromassage showers) make it the first choice of many celebrities. Roof-top swimming pool (see p59). ✪ Gran Vía 53 • Map P2 • 91 547 2800 • www.emperadorhotel.com • Dis. access • €€€

El Botánico
This discrete 3-star hotel has a stunning Sierra backdrop. The tasteful rooms are equipped with satellite TV. The hotel has a restaurant, garage and meeting rooms. ✪ Calle Timoteo Padrós 16, San Lorenzo de El Escorial • Map A1 • 91 890 7879 • www.botanicohotel.com • €€

General Index

Acknowledgements

Main Contributors

Christopher and Melanie Rice have travelled throughout Europe, writing travel guides to destinations from the Algarve to the Turkish Coast. They were main contributors to Dorling Kindersley's Eyewitness guides to Moscow and St Petersburg. The Rices have been visiting Madrid for more than 20 years and have now decided to make it their home.

Produced by Sargasso Media Ltd, London
Project Editor Zoë Ross
Art Editors Philip Lord, Janis Utton
Picture Research Monica Allende, Marta Bescos, Ellen Root
Proofreader Stewart J Wild
Indexer Hilary Bird

Main Photographer
Peter Wilson

Additional Photography
Marta Bescos, Heidi Grassley, Neil Lukas, Isabel Real Martinez, Kim Sayer

Illustrator
Chris Orr & Associates

FOR DORLING KINDERSLEY
Publishing Managers Jane Ewart, Fay Franklin
Publisher Douglas Amrine
Cartography Co-ordinator Casper Morris
DTP Jason Little
Production Sarah Dodd
Maps James Anderson, Jane Voss (Anderson Geographics, Berks)
Editorial Assistance Cristina Barrallo, Laura Edgecumbe, Anna Freiberger, Lydia Halliday, Integrated Publishing Solutions, Juliet Kenny, Maite Lantaron, Kate Molan, Edward Owen, Andrea Pinnington, Quadrum Solutions, Rada Radojicic, Susana Smith, Conrad Van Dyk

Picture Credits

a = above; b = below/bottom; c = centre; f = far; l = left; r = right; t = top.

Every effort has been made to trace the copyright holders, and we apologize in advance for any unintentional omissions. We would be pleased to insert the appropriate acknowledgements in any subsequent edition of this publication.

The publishers would like to thank the following individuals, companies, and picture libraries for permission to reproduce their photographs:

© DACS 2011 "*Meeting place*" by Chillida 57t, 81t.

AISA, Barcelona: 1, 4–5, 6cb, 7br, 9cr, 10tl, 10b, 11c, 11b, 36cb, 36b, 37t, 36–7, 37cb, 38tl, 38tr, 40tl, 40tr, 40ca, 40b, 41tr, 41br,42b, © Successio Miro, DACS 2011 44tl, 44tr, 47t, 51b, 54tl, 70–71, 97t, 97b, 118–19, 124tr, 125t, "*The Adoration of the Shepherds*" by El Greco 12ca, "*Still Life with Pottery Jars*" by Zurbaran 12b, "*Las Meninas*" by Diego Velázquez 13ca, "*The Meadow of St Isidore*" by Goya 13b, "*The Story of Nastagio degli Onesti*" by Botticelli 14tl, "*Annunciation*" by

Fra Angelico 14tr, "*David with the Head of Goliath*" by Caravaggio 14b, "*The Third of May 1808*" by Goya 15b, © DACS 2011 "*The Gathering at Café de Pombo*" by Jose Gutierrez Solana 28-29, "*The Martyrdom of St Maurice and the Theban Legion*" by El Greco 38b, "*Calvary*" by Rogier van der Weyden 39t, "*Portrait of Felipe II*" by Titian 39b; ALMAY IMAGES: Kevin Foy 28–29c; Hemis 30 tr; Richard Naude 140tl; ALDEASA. ES: 132tl; ALICE IN WONDER-LAND: 121tr.

CALLE54: 60br; CAIXA FORUM MADRID. FUNDACION LA CAIXA: 92tl; MUSEO NACIONAL CENTRO DE ARTE REINA SOFIA: Joaquín Cortés 28bl; © Successio Miro, DACS 2011 "*Portrait II*" by Joan Miro 7tr, 29tr, © ADAGP, Paris and DACS, London 2011 "*Guitar in Front of the Sea*" by Juan Gris 29cr, "*Accident*" by Alfonso Ponce de Leon 29bl, © DACS 2011 "*Toki-Egin*" Chillida 30tl, © Succession Picasso/DACS 2011 "*Guernica*" by Picasso 31b; COVER, Madrid: 42tl, 42tr, 43t, 43r, 51t, 54tr, 54b, 55t, 59t.

ESTADO PURO: 68bl.

GETTY IMAGES: The Bridgeman Art Library 13tc.

HORIZONTAL: 128tr.

MARCO POLO, Madrid: 52b, 58tl, 58b, 129t; MUSEO DE AMERICA: 7b, 34cb, 34b, 35t, 35ca, 35b; MUSEO THYSSEN BORNEMISZA: "*Portrait of a Young Man*" by Raphael 7ca, 25b, "*Christ and Woman of Samaria at the Well*" by Buoninsegna 24b, "*The Annunciation*" by El Greco 25t, "*Woman with a Parasol in a Garden*" by Renoir 26tl, "*Les Vessenots*" by Van Gogh 26tr, "*Swaying Dancer*" by Degas 26b, "*Hotel Room*" by Hopper 27b.

PATRIMONIO NACIONAL: 6t, 6b, 8-9, 8b, 9t, 9b, 10tr, 10ca, 20–21, 21cr, 21clb, 21b.

RAMON FREIXA MADRID: 69tr; RENFE: 133tl; RESTAURANTE BOTIN: 113tl; RESTAURANTE CHAROLES: 128tl.

SPECTRUM COLOUR LIBRARY: 130–31; SUPERSTOCK: AGE fotostock 114tr.

TELEFONICA: 140tr.

PETER WILSON: 90–91.

All other images are © DK. For further information see www.dkimages.com

Phrase Book

In an Emergency

Help!	**¡Socorro!**	soh-koh-roh
Stop!	**¡Pare!**	pah-reh
Call a doctor!	**¡Llame a un médico!**	yah-meh ah oon meh-dee-koh
Call an ambulance!	**¡Llame a una ambulancia!**	yah-meh ah oonah ahm-boo-lahn-thee-ah
Call the police!	**¡Llame a la policía!**	yah-meh ah lah poh-lee-thee-ah
Call the fire brigade!	**¡Llame a los bomberos!**	yah-meh ah lohs bohm-beh-rohs
Where is the nearest telephone?	**¿Dónde está el teléfono más próximo?**	dohn-deh ehs-tah teh-leh-foh-noh mahs prohx-ee moh
Where is the nearest hospital?	**¿Dónde está el hospital más próximo?**	dohn-deh ehs-tah ehl ohs-pee-tahl mahs prohx-ee-moh

Communication Essentials

Yes	**Sí**	see
No	**No**	noh
Please	**Por favor**	pohr fah-vohr
Thank you	**Gracias**	grah-thee-ahs
Excuse me	**Perdone**	pehr-doh-neh
Hello	**Hola**	oh-lah
Goodbye	**Adiós**	ah-dee-ohs
Good night	**Buenas noches**	bweh-nahs noh-chehs
Morning	**La mañana**	lah mah-nyah-nah
Afternoon	**La tarde**	lah tahr-deh
Evening	**La tarde**	lah tahr-deh
Yesterday	**Ayer**	ah-yehr
Today	**Hoy**	oy
Tomorrow	**Mañana**	mah-nya-nah
Here	**Aquí**	ah-kee
There	**Allí**	ah-yee
What?	**¿Qué?**	keh
When?	**¿Cuándo?**	kwahn-doh
Why?	**¿Por qué?**	pohr-keh
Where?	**¿Dónde?**	dohn-deh

Useful Phrases

How are you?	**¿Cómo está usted?**	koh-moh ehs-tah oos-tehd
Very well, thank you	**Muy bien, gracias**	mwee bee-ehn grah-thee-ahs
Pleased to meet you.	**Encantado de conocerle.**	ehn-kahn-tah-doh deh koh-noh-thehr-leh
See you soon	**Hasta pronto**	ahs-tah prohn-toh
That's fine	**Está bien**	ehs-tah bee-ehn
Where is/are...?	**¿Dónde está/están...?**	dohn-deh ehs-tah/ehs-tahn
How far is it to...?	**¿Cuántos metros/ kilómetros hay de aquí a...?**	kwahn-tohs meh-trohs/kee-loh-meh-trohs eye deh ah-kee ah
Which way to...?	**¿Por dónde se va a...?**	pohr dohn-deh seh bah ah
Do you speak English?	**¿Habla inglés?**	ah-blah een-glehs
I don't understand	**No comprendo**	noh kohm-prehn-doh
Could you speak more slowly please?	**¿Puede hablar más despacio por favor?**	pweh-deh ah-blahr mahs dehs-pah-thee-oh pohr fah-vohr
I'm sorry	**Lo siento**	loh see-ehn-toh

Useful Words

big	**grande**	grahn-deh
small	**pequeño**	peh-keh-nyoh
hot	**caliente**	kah-lee-ehn-teh
cold	**frío**	free-oh
good	**bueno**	bweh-noh
bad	**malo**	mah-loh
enough	**bastante**	bahs-tahn-teh
well	**bien**	bee-ehn
open	**abierto**	ah-bee-ehr-toh
closed	**cerrado**	thehr-rah-doh
left	**izquierda**	eeth-key-ehr-dah
right	**derecha**	deh-reh-chah
straight on	**todo recto**	toh-doh rehk-toh
near	**cerca**	thehr-kah

far	**lejos**	leh-hohs
up	**arriba**	ah-ree-bah
down	**abajo**	ah-bah-hoh
early	**temprano**	tehm-prah-noh
late	**tarde**	tahr-deh
entrance	**entrada**	ehn-trah-dah
exit	**salida**	sah-lee-dah
toilet	**lavabos, servicios**	lah-vah-bohs, sehr-bee-thee-ohs
more	**más**	mahs
less	**menos**	meh-nohs

Shopping

How much does this cost?	**¿Cuánto cuesta esto?**	kwahn-toh kwehs-tah ehs-toh
I would like...	**Me gustaría...**	meh goos-ta-ree-ah
Do you have?	**¿Tienen?**	tee-yeh-nehn
I'm just looking	**Sólo estoy mirando**	soh-loh ehs-toy mee-rahn-doh
Do you take credit cards?	**¿Aceptan tarjetas de crédito?**	ah-thehp-tahn tahr-heh-tahs deh kreh-dee-toh
What time do you open?	**¿A qué hora abren?**	ah keh oh-rah ah-brehn
What time do you close?	**¿A qué hora cierran?**	ah keh oh-rah thee-eh-rrahn
This one	**Éste**	ehs-teh
That one	**Ése**	eh-seh
expensive	**caro**	kahr-oh
cheap	**barato**	bah-rah-toh
size, clothes	**talla**	tah-yah
size, shoes	**número**	noo-mehr-oh
white	**blanco**	blahn-koh
black	**negro**	neh-groh
red	**rojo**	roh-hoh
yellow	**amarillo**	ah-mah-ree-yoh
green	**verde**	behr-deh
blue	**azul**	ah-thool
antiques shop	**la tienda de antigüedades**	lah tee-ehn-dah deh ahn-tee-gweh-dah-dehs
bakery	**la panadería**	lah pah-nah-deh-ree-ah
bank	**el banco**	ehl bahn-koh
bookshop	**la librería**	lah lee-breh-ree-ah
butcher's	**la carnicería**	lah kar-nee-theh-ree-ah
cake shop	**la pastelería**	lah pahs-teh-leh-ree-ah
chemist's	**la farmacia**	lah fahr-mah-thee-ah
fishmonger's	**la pescadería**	lah pehs-kah-deh-ree-ah
greengrocer's	**la frutería**	lah froo-teh-ree-ah
grocer's	**la tienda de comestibles**	lah tee-yehn-dah deh koh-mehs-tee-blehs
hairdresser's	**la peluquería**	lah peh-loo-keh-ree-ah
market	**el mercado**	ehl mehr-kah-doh
newsagent's	**el kiosko de prensa**	ehl kee-ohs-koh deh prehn-sah
post office	**la oficina de correos**	lah oh-fee-thee-nah deh kohr-reh-ohs
shoe shop	**la zapatería**	lah thah-pah-teh-ree-ah
supermarket	**el supermercado**	ehl soo-pehr-mehr-kah-doh
tobacconist	**el estanco**	ehl ehs-tahn-koh
travel agency	**la agencia de viajes**	lah ah-hehn-thee-ah deh bee-ah-hehs

Sightseeing

art gallery	**el museo de arte**	ehl moo-seh-oh deh ahr-teh
cathedral	**la catedral**	lah kah-teh-drahl
church	**la iglesia**	lah ee-gleh-see-ah
	la basílica	lah bah-see-lee-kah
garden	**el jardín**	ehl hahr-deen
library	**la biblioteca**	lah bee-blee-oh-teh-kah
museum	**el museo**	ehl moo-seh-oh
tourist information office	**la oficina de turismo**	lah oh-fee-thee nah deh too-rees-moh
town hall	**el ayuntamiento**	ehl ah-yoon-toh mee-ehn-toh
closed for holiday	**cerrado por vacaciones**	thehr-rah-doh pohr bah-kah-thee-oh-nehs
bus station	**la estación de autobuses**	lah ehs-tah-thee-ohn deh owtoh-boo-sehs
railway station	**la estación de trenes**	lah ehs-tah-thee-ohn deh treh-nehs